Visions of Architecture

S T E P H E N L E E S

A&C Black · London

First published in Great Britain 2011
A&C Black Publishers
36 Soho Square
London W1D 3QY
www.acblack.com

ISBN: 978-1-4081-2881-7

A CIP catalogue record for this book is available
from the British Library

Page design: Evelin Kasikov
Cover design: Sutchinda Thompson
Commissioning editor: Linda Lambert
Copy editor: Julian Beecroft
Proofreader: Ellen Parnavelas

This book is produced using paper
that is made from wood grown in
managed, sustainable forests. It is
natural, renewable and recyclable.
The logging and manufacturing
processes conform to the environmental
regulations of the country of origin.

Printed in China by C&C Offset Printing Co. Ltd

Frontispiece
Fig. 1. *Proposal for New Colony Room Building*
Though only a proposed concept, this isometric drawing
shows how a building can be designed to dominate an
area. The building's mass and proportions are clearly
represented in the proposed structure. The design takes
into account the practical and aesthetic requirements of
the existing Club in Dean Street, London.

PREFACE

This book is my vision and interpretation of 52 buildings I have drawn and reproduced here. Focusing on interesting design details, I set each of these structures in its political and economic context, which readers may not be aware of, though they are familiar with the structures themselves. I identify the reasons for their design and creation in the light of the major developments in architecture, civil engineering, religion and the arts of the time.

The buildings are expressed as architectural line drawings that reveal their structural and architectural features in detail. Interpreting buildings by drawing them is an effective way of understanding the design concepts that went into their creation and the hidden influence they exert on their immediate environment.

The range of buildings covered is wide and their method and circumstances of construction are often fascinating. Among other matters, I consider how the first mausoleums, including the pyramids developed by ancient civilisations, initiated the architectural revolution whose results affect us to this day; how other less dramatic but equally huge concrete structures were able to perform acts such as rolling over onto their backs; why a room in a New York railroad station, known as 'the largest room in the world', was merely a waiting room; how, were it not for the pyramid temple designs of the ancient Mayan civilisation, we would not have the distinctive Art Deco style of the Empire State Building and other structures built during the 1930s; and how this remarkable building ever came to be constructed – not as a sensible property development, but as a result of intense rivalry between two megalomaniacs.

I also examine how the use of new materials allowed each generation of builders to extend the scope and size of buildings ranging from the ancient Acropolis to modern railroad stations, and from concrete bunkers to skyscrapers; how the hydraulic engine enabled builders to construct massive structures and build skyscrapers to unprecedented heights; how the design of those skyscrapers was based on a method of construction invented by the Victorians which ultimately saved the Empire State Building from collapse when a plane flew into it (unlike the fate that befell the World Trade Center towers in New York); how despite that brilliant design innovation the same Victorians applied this method of construction primarily to the construction Gothic buildings based on fantasy, but providing consolation for their terror of death.

Stephen Lees
Chicago, September 2010

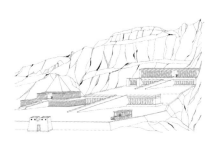

LIST OF ILLUSTRATIONS

INTRODUCTION

Why are buildings important to us?

Buildings are important to us, as we spend a significant proportion of our lives inside them. A successful building is regarded as a structure that meets our needs, and we are not disposed to experiment with something as important as our home. The style, shape, size, colour and location of buildings are of concern to us, and dominate how we think about our environment.

When we design buildings we impose our collective psyche on the built environment, which includes preferences over what we consider aesthetically acceptable. As a result, change – for instance, in how a building is constructed – happens slowly and is often resisted at first. But once a particular style has come to be accepted, it can develop a language full of meaning. For example, churches, government bodies, commercial companies and so on create buildings that are a generally recognisable 'type' that allows their ready identification; in its design is represented the building's purpose, and in some cases also the wealth and, by implication, the power and success of its creator.

Yet the meaning of buildings cannot be fixed permanently. For example, today cathedrals are widely regarded as places of understanding and tolerance, but in the Middle Ages they were powerful centres of social control. Buildings can inspire a range of feelings in the beholder – from intimidation, unease and foreboding to relief and comfort, or even indifference. These impressions may sometimes seem ill-fitted to the building in question, and may not even have been intended by the architect.

For example, the design of fig. 34 (see p.76), a temple in California, brings more to mind the architecture and symbolism of a fortress than it does a place of peace and contemplation. The whole edifice is massive and built upon a high plinth allowing access only through narrow steps that lead to the interior. The design suggests the temple's massive solidity, expressed in hard and defined masonry blocks of white granite complete with dark recesses forming window reveals to the upper section of the temple.

This is an example of a building that, it can be argued, does not to look 'right' for its purpose. So why was it made that way? This book sets out to explore why buildings are made to look the way they do, and the impressions they may have on us, whether intended or incidental. The first chapter considers the ancient Egyptians and Greeks, who imposed their thoughts, feelings and ambitions on their environment with such force and vision that they have had an enduring impact on Western architecture. Having set the scene, the rest of the book goes on to explore the last 300 years of Western architecture. It considers the aspirations of the makers of buildings: from the wealthy 18th-century megalomaniac William Beckford (see p.108–10), to the corporations who constructed skyscrapers in 20th-century New York (see p.87–97), and everything in between. It also investigates how buildings are made, from innovations in construction, to the impact of new materials and technologies from the Industrial Revolution to the modern day.

CHAPTER I

Ancient Egypt: the beginning

The Egyptians initiated the architectural 'Big Bang'. With the pyramids – one of the earliest surviving forms of the mausoleum – the ancient Egyptians initiated an evolution of architecture that led to the use of stone in the construction of important buildings. In doing so they created the foundations of Western architecture based on durable stone. The ancient Egyptians started the cult of housing the dead, for reasons that made perfect sense to them and their religious culture. They believed that when the god Osiris was killed by his brother Cect, he was embalmed and resurrected as the god of the dead. His son, the god Horus, reincarnated himself as a god on earth residing within the body of the living Pharaoh.

From this event developed the need to prepare a dead Pharaoh for the celestial afterlife, his divine prerogative. This necessitated the construction of a structure, a mausoleum, in which to house the Pharaoh along with his splendour and wealth for eternity. This meant using materials of a more permanent nature, such as the limestone and granite that were plentiful in Egypt, rather than timber or mud brick. This fact was the motivating factor behind the construction of the pyramids and their auxiliary mortuary temple buildings in the Nile Valley.

In this respect the desire for grand mausoleum structures was the spark that caused the architectural innovation that led to construction using masonry to form vertical columns to receive a horizontal stone beam.

Advances made in architecture and construction methods were intense. With no previous experience to draw upon, the Egyptians had to deal with the problem of how to build massive monolithic structures that would last for millennia. Among the first attempts to carry out this desire for the eternal was the construction *c*.3000BC of the Mastaba, a 9m (30ft) high flat-topped tomb structure with sloping external walls built of mud brick. The transition from the Mastaba, an early form of short pyramid structure, to the more formal, angular stepped stone pyramid is evident in the building constructed to house the dead Pharaoh Zoser in 2750BC at Saqqara, the huge necropolis located near Memphis, the capital of ancient Egypt. Adjacent to that stepped pyramid were auxiliary buildings, including mortuary temples, vestibule buildings, the Massima temples, Hypostyle halls, sanctuaries and offering chapel of funereal rites. These buildings were located within a 10m (33ft) high walled enclosure called the Precinct – the domain of the gods – entry into which was through an entrance building called the Pylon. These cult buildings adjacent to the pyramid were connected by an elevated ceremonial causeway leading from the valley building containing the preparation chapels where the embalming of deceased Pharaohs took place. This building in turn was connected to the River Nile by means of a canal along which the elaborate funeral cortège made its way. These buildings indicate clearly the predilection of the ancient Egyptians for monumental structures of stone that were built to last.

Fig. 2. *Mortuary Temples of Mentuhotep II, at Luxor, 21st century BC, Mentuhotep II*

Several Pharaohs contributed funerary structures to this sacred necropolis at Deir el-Bahari, known as the 'Sublime of Sublimes'. In particular, the powerful Pharaoh Mentuhotep II built several structures here, including the small pyramid elevated on the colonnaded podium, which was his cenotaph, whilst his body was interned deeply in the adjacent mountain rock. Five hundred years' later, Queen Hatshepsut constructed the elaborate series of terraces regressing into the granite mountains which contain the burial chambers of the Pharaohs. Access to this walled necropolis was via the monumental Pylon entrance building visible at the bottom left.

The construction of Deir ei-Bahari represented a balancing act between the evolution of construction skills and the requirements of religious protocol. The range of structures demanded to satisfy the Pharaohs' prerogative in the provision of eternal structures was diverse – from sacred houses such as the elegant Mammisa Temple (seen here at the bottom right-hand corner) to impressive terraces of limestone – and demonstrates the skill developed by ancient Egyptian builders.

The names of these innovative stone structures are still in common use today, which is one demonstration of the influence of the ancient Egyptians on the development of architecture.

After this first step, the need to construct temples for different uses drove the development of the architecture of different building forms incorporating different requirements. All involved stone structures of colossal weight, and development was slow and methodical. For example, in the necropolis at Saqqara *c.*2750BC the interior stone ceiling of a temple is supported by a series of half columns. These semicircular columns are attached to adjoining piers, short stone walls connecting the columns to the main walls of the temple. Using this method of construction the Egyptians hoped to attain a safe margin by which the columns could cope with the massive and heavy stone vault roof. The Egyptians, at this stage did not dare to build freestanding columns to receive this weight.

The construction methods evolved by the ancient Egyptians represent the first formal systematic application of architectural principles, later adapted by the ancient Greeks and later still by the Romans. For example, the papyrus plant, prized by the ancient Egyptians for its beauty and symbolism, was used in the design of capitals located on the top of columns. The leaves of the plant when in bloom splay outward. Represented in stone this natural design allowed capitals to receive the end of a horizontal stone beam on a greater area – a technical solution that was also an aesthetic enhancement – creating a more secure base. The design of this masonry capital was used by the ancient Greeks and became known as the Doric order of capital (see p.14). Similarly, Greek architects took up the idea of the pylon, a monumental entrance structure with four inclined, decorated walls with a gateway opening. An example exists at the Mortuary Temple complex of Mentuhotep II at Deir el-Bahari near Thebes, dating from 2065BC (opposite).

One hundred and ten pyramids were constructed in ancient Egypt using stone blocks. These ancient tombs are complex structures, incorporating corridors, voids, chambers, crypts and access door openings, which necessitated the rapid evolution of structural engineering to handle the prodigious weights and forces involved. Whilst transporting heavy stone blocks and manipulating them into position, the builders also had to contend with creating access corridors to voids and burial chambers formed within the stone structure of the pyramid. Creating voids was potentially a lethal exercise, as understanding of the mechanics of dead weight was still fairly basic.

A large internal chamber could have a ceiling comprised of stone corbelling. In such a construction the ceiling roof is made up of courses of stone blocks which at each ascending layer step inward from the walls of the chamber, in effect creating an apex ceiling shell in the form of a hollow pyramid supporting the considerable weight of the structure above. If internal forces move out of line within the structure, as they might when the building settles, this could trigger an internal collapse as the constructional forces seek out the lines of least resistance. Placing a stone block on top of another stone block is a safe and predictable form of construction. However, where several thousand stone blocks are positioned upon each other, a colossal weight is produced creating unimaginable compression forces acting within the pyramid through those blocks.

In the case of most of the pyramids, these compressive forces were successfully harnessed for construction purposes – but not all, notably one at Meidum completed in 2704BC, known as 'the collapsed pyramid'. Indeed, some were abandoned or became too unsafe for the workers to complete, while others fell into disuse, their stone removed for work on other pyramids. The pyramid at Dashur suffered a partial internal collapse which left a distinctive bent attitude to its profile. Normally, the sides of a pyramid are

Fig. 3.

The Acropolis, Athens, c.440 BC,
Pericles and Phidias

A drawing of how the monumental and
ceremonial complex of temples of the
Acropolis may have looked. From left
to right can be seen the temples of
Erechtheion, Propylaea and Nike Apteros,
all subject to the dominating splendour and
majesty of the Parthenon temple dedicated
to Athena at the far right.

straight; not so at Dashur, where halfway up the
pyramid the projected angle of construction of
54 degrees is abruptly altered to a less steep angle
of 43 degrees, indicating structural turmoil
within the pyramid and the builders' subsequent
attempt to correct it.

Pyramid building culminated in the Great
Pyramid of Giza *c.*2560BC, for the Pharaoh
Cheops. This massive pyramid weighing
15 million tons took over 30 years to build and
used many workers, in excess of 100,000 at the
height of construction. The base of the pyramid
was an area of 13 acres and rose from the desert
floor to an unprecedented 146m (480ft). This
made it the tallest built structure on earth –
a record it retained for over 4,500 years – and
earned it its place as one of the Seven Wonders
of the Ancient World. The Egyptians went to
this length in building huge structures literally
to attain immortality on the basis that the
bigger the building the longer it would last.

Pyramids were constructed not in isolation but
as a group in a complex of funerary buildings
all contained within a walled temporal enclosure
and known as a necropolis. This area was
reserved as a domain of the gods. This idea
was used by the Greeks when constructing their
Acropolis two thousand years later in Athens
(see p.8–10). During his reign, in 1301BC, the
Pharaoh Ramesses II completed the magnificent
temples at Abu Simbel. On the front elevation of
the mortuary temples, guarding the entrances,
and carved into the red sandstone are four
super-monumental statues of Ramesses II,
all 20m (67ft) tall. The interior of the temple
was created by cutting into the rock itself.
Over 36.5m (120ft) in length and 14m (45ft)
in height, the rock walls of the temple are
buttressed by stupendous monuments in the
form of giant statues of the god Osiris.

✺ Abandoning the mighty pyramids

Eventually the pyramid form of construction to house dead Pharaohs fell out of favour. Instead corridors were tunnelled into the living rock to create a crypt tomb, discreet burial chambers fronted by a magnificent monumental colonnaded limestone screen, the mortuary temple.

The most sacred was the temple complex of the Pharaohs called Deir-el-Bahari, meaning 'The Northern Monastery', which is located on the west bank of the River Nile opposite the ancient capital of Luxor. Known as the 'Sublime of Sublimes', its construction by Mentuhotep II began in 2065BC, with a tunnel being driven into the granite rock cliffs of the Nile Valley. Later, in 1277BC, the Pharaoh Seti built the most sacred of all mortuary temples. Located at Abydos the temple was dedicated to the god Osiris for his role in helping the Pharaohs successfully complete their journey to the hereafter. This temple complex of limestone columns set in

a terrace of colonnades shows the importance attached to the cult of death endorsed by the Pharaohs. The elaborate doubled-storied colonnade at Deir-el-Bahari was added by the Pharaoh Queen Hatshepsut in 1520BC, complete with monumental ramps leading to the interior, which was cut into the rock cliff immediately behind the mortuary temple complex and in which the burial chambers were secretly located inside a labyrinth. Also within the precinct of this temple complex is a stone pyramid laid out on the second inset platform, which supported a colonnaded podium and acted as a cenotaph, an empty mausoleum and a focus for worship of the dead Pharaoh. The form of this pyramid, if viewed from its ceremonial front elevation, resembles the mausoleum that was later built at Halicarnassus by the Greeks in 355–350BC. Again the Greeks learnt from the Egyptians how to construct their own iconic monumental temples and buildings.

Fig. 4.

The Erechtheion, Athens, c.405BC,
Mnesicles

Located on the Acropolis, this temple by
Erechteus, King of Athens, was constructed
of white Pentelic marble with a black
Eleusinian limestone frieze. Due to the
temple having to accommodate existing
sacred burial sites, it was built with
an irregular design on two distinct levels,
and incorporated three porches and
an attached colonnade.

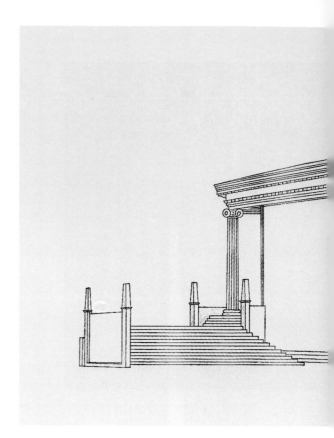

The evolution of the mausoleum and its impact
on the development of architecture continued
with the construction of the mausoleum built
at Halicarnassos in *c.*350BC. Commissioned
by Artemisia, the widow of King Mausolos, to
remember him for eternity, this was a massive
classical building measuring 44m (145ft) high,
27m (89ft) wide and 36.5m (120ft) long, which
ensured that it would come to be ranked as one
of the Seven Wonders of the Ancient World.
The building also established the prototype
for all succeeding mortuary temples to the
dead. It was a monumental structure designed
deliberately for a clear and unequivocal purpose
– to express the immortality of the dead person.
The elevated podium of the mausoleum was
surrounded by 36 columns of the Ionic order
surmounted by a stepped pyramid.

❦ Ancient Greece: honouring the gods

Where the Egyptians had built monumentally
to ensure the safe passage of their dead rulers
to the afterlife, the Greeks used the Egyptian
advances in mausoleum construction to erect
temples to honour their living gods. The temples
that comprise the Acropolis complex in Athens
were constructed by the rulers of the Athenian
state to affirm their belief in and adoration
of the Olympian gods. The temples include the
Erechtheion built by Erechtheus, the ancient
King of Athens; the Propylaea, the monumental
gateway; the Pinacotheca, the hall of fame;
and the temple of Athena Nike Apteros (Nike
meaning 'victory'), which overlooks the Straits of
Salamis, the scene of Athens' naval victory over
the Persian fleet in 480BC. Chief amongst the
temples is the magnificent Parthenon constructed
by Pericles. It was dedicated to the goddess
Athena Parthenos, patron deity of Athens,
as a palatial shrine to commemorate the city's

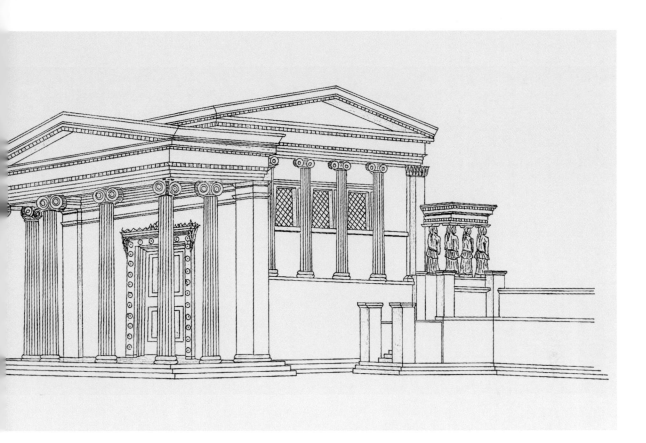

deliverance from war. It was also used as the treasury for the wealth of the Athenian city-state.

The Acropolis is perhaps the most important group of buildings to have influenced Western civilisation and architecture. This complex of temples was constructed as a symbol of the emerging power of Athens after it had successfully dealt with the Persians, and celebrates Athens' enhanced role in the new world order of the time.

This walled citadel of the Acropolis, in which the temples were constructed on a stone-covered plaza, is located on a natural plateau of rock. The Acropolis, which means 'city of heights' was accessible only via the broad monumental flight of steps ascending the hill leading to the Propylaea entrance. That structure defined the boundary between the public, secular realm and the sacred buildings of the gods, and to an extent was based on the ancient Egyptian concept of the necropolis, the separate domain

of their gods, entry into which was via the Pylon, the equivalent of the Propylaea.

The general layout of the Acropolis site and the detailed designs of the various temples were the result of the new science of geometry being developed by Pythagoras and the advances made in mathematical logic. In this respect the inherent beauty of the vision of this collection of temples was based not purely on instinctive aesthetics, but rather on a new aesthetic sensibility based on geometrical calculation, which dictated the position, size, shape and structure of the temples.

The temples that make up the Acropolis were built of white Pentelic marble blocks upon a crepidoma of three or more steps. The solidity of the buildings' construction and the precision of the joints between the separate marble blocks, none of which involve the use of mortar, have enabled the buildings to remain standing for over 2,500 years. It is probable that the temples would have been even more intact than they are, were it not for the systematic vandalism meted out to them by later, successive occupiers of Athens.

Whilst the Parthenon is the largest of the temples, the Erechtheion was the focus of the adoration of the Olympian gods, several of whom could be worshipped within its confines. The temple was divided into distinct areas for worship of the different gods, and this was reflected in its base floor areas. These were dedicated to Zeus, supreme in the pantheon of the Olympian deities, and Poseidon, god of the oceans, while the upper floor was reserved for the shrine to Athena Polias, goddess of the Athenian city-state.

The Erechtheion evolved from a previous ancient temple structure, with annexes being added over the years. However, in order to show respect for the original temple and its symbolism, the Erechtheion temple developed into an unusual configuration with different floor levels to accommodate existing altars and tombs. This accounts for the peculiar floor levels throughout the building and its asymmetrical layout, which nevertheless do not detract from its astonishing beauty.

A notable feature on the Erechtheion is a group of statues depicting the Caryatids. These female draped marble figures, supporting the porch on the south side of the building, are said to represent the priestesses from the island of Caryatis, who, having sided with the Persians against Athens, were enslaved and metamorphosed into marble. They face the Parthenon as a warning to all mortals to maintain their loyalty to the goddess Athena and to Athens. There is a full-size replica of the Porch of the Caryatids at the church of St Pancras, built in 1822, opposite the St Pancras Hotel in London.

The 13m (42ft) high gold-plated statue of Athena Parthenos, sculpted by Pheidias, shows her on a pedestal, armed with a spear, wearing a helmet and holding an aegis supporting winged Victory in her hand. The prospect of beholding a 13m (42ft) high gold-plated statue of a Greek goddess may seem daunting, but this super-monumental scale for statues was considered normal at the time for adorning huge temples.

The sculptor Pheidias was renowned for covering his creations in gold and ivory (or chryselephantine, to give this combination its proper name). These included the colossal statue of Zeus at the Temple of Olympia, another of the Seven Wonders, and Promachos, a bronze colossus that took nine years to complete and towered above the Parthenon and Erechtheion. Though their statues for the inner sanctum were of colossal proportions, the Greeks managed to avoid the architectural megalomania practised by the earlier Egyptians as well as later civilisations when constructing their structures.

Copies of Greek temples are to be found throughout the Western world. The Lincoln Memorial (begun 1911) and the Temple of Freemasonry Rite (begun 1911), both modelled on the Mausoleum of Halicarnassos, can be found in Washington, DC; the Parthenon temple, complete with a full-size statue of the goddess Athena Parthenon, can be seen at Nashville, Tennessee. In Bavaria in the mid-19th century Leo von Klenze copied the Parthenon in his Valhalla temple near Regensburg (completed in 1842) and also replicated the Propylaea in Munich (completed in 1862). A variation of the Parthenon design is evident at both the Schauspielhaus in Berlin (completed in 1821) and the British Museum in London (completed in 1847). Three other notable buildings that apply the classical orders of Doric, Corinthian and Ionic respectively are the Euston Arch in London (see p.106–7) (demolished in the 1960s), St George's Hall in Liverpool and the aforementioned Temple of Freemasonry Rite, Washington, DC.

Fig. 5.
Temple of Freemasonry Rite,
Washington, DC, 1911, John Pope

This Temple is based on the
original Mausoleum built in 350 BC
at Halicarnassos for King Mausolos.
The Temple is a faithful reconstruction
of the Mausoleum, expressing the sheer
size and magnificence of the original
building. Constructed 2,360 years ago,
it was the first Mausoleum to be built
in the classical style, and was the model
for succeeding Mortuary Temples.

Fig. 6.

Schauspielhaus, Berlin,
1820, Karl von Schinkel

Created by Karl von Schinkel in 1819 as
a powerful exposition of the Greek Revival
style, the Schauspielhaus represents
a double Parthenon expressed in a series
of rectangular shapes.

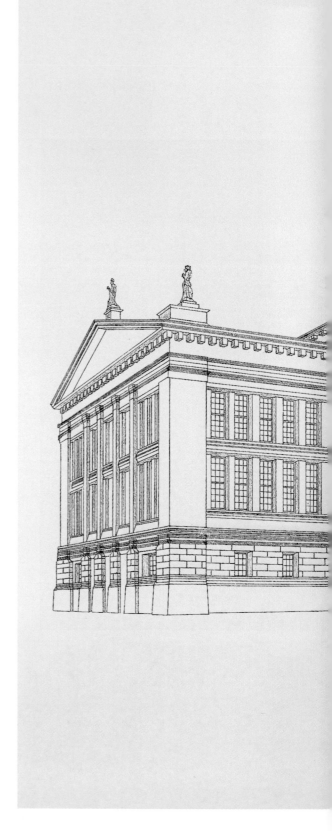

❧ The basic structure of a classical building

The Greeks used three orders of architecture in construction: the masculine Doric order represented at the Parthenon; the slender feminine Ionic order typified at the Erechtheion (see pp.8–9); and the later Corinthian order with its marked ornate floral relief to the capital at the top of the column, adopted by the Romans in constructing their imperial buildings. Connecting the tops of each column is the horizontal masonry, the entablature. This stone beam is comprised of the architrave (the lower part), the frieze (the middle part) and the cornice (the upper part).

Typically, the construction of a classical building or temple would follow certain precepts. A plinth comprising two layers of steps, the crepidoma, would be laid out to receive the final stepped plinth, the stylobate, forming a rectangular platform area with longitudinal sides. Low vertical square blocks, the pedestals, would be positioned on the stylobate along the front, back and the two sides of the stepped platform. Then a circular curved stone drum, the base, would be anchored on each of these pedestals. Narrower stone drums placed on top of each other would be positioned upon this curved base, rising vertically to form a series of columns, a colonnade. These colonnades in turn created the front, back and side views, the elevations, of the edifice being constructed. The columns would be terminated at the top with capitals. Upon these capitals a stone beam was laid, the entablature, which connected each column to the adjacent column forming a bridge and stone frame, which bridged the entire colonnade and completed the basic structure of the building. The entablature was made up of three distinct parts. The lower part, the architrave, was usually made of undecorated smooth marble. Resting upon the architrave would be the decorative marble frieze. This was a series of carved stone slabs, metopes, usually featuring detailed representations of gods and mortals in relief,

and set back between a series of projecting marble piers carved with vertical grooves, or triglyphs, which connected the architrave to the cornice. The cornice was the prominent upper most part of the entablature stone beam and was wider than any part of the front or back of the building constructed so far beneath it. The cornice would overhang the architrave and frieze, ready to receive the pediment, a low triangular-shaped stone frame the width of which was usually seven times its height. Into this recessed pediment the tympanum was carved, again adorned with decorative marble relief. Finally, at the edge and top of the pediment were positioned the Acroterion, carved statues or stone representations of floral designs or wings.

The most immediate aspect of Greek architecture is the well-thought-out geometric pattern to which their buildings conform, creating a pleasing symmetry. Most of their buildings were open, meaning that they integrated easily into the wider public space, known as the Agora.

Temples were buildings for the gods not places of worship. Because the temples were windowless and roofed and thus the interior was dark accordingly, worship did not take place inside. The design of a temple was focused not on the interior but rather on the exterior, complete with statues adorning stepped pedestals forming shrines to the deities to whom the temple was dedicated. Chief among these shrines would be the altar, which was pivotal in the conduct of rituals involving the Olympian gods.

Fig. 7.

Fantasy Perspective

This drawing of a imaginary temple interior explores the use of Pythagorean geometry to represent distance and perspective in an ethereal but opulent scene of the Classical orders.

❀ The legacy of ancient Egyptian and Greek architecture

Both the ancient Egyptians and the Greeks left numerous architectural mechanisms from which we have developed certain building techniques. The original idea of the sloped, stepped Mastaba tomb is repeated in the design of the Cenotaph at Whitehall in London. That same design was applied extensively when constructing the massive Art Deco buildings during the 20th century such as the US Federal Bullion Reserve (see pp.83–4), or the Museum of Contemporary Art in Sydney, Australia. The first column, at the mortuary temple of the Pharaoh Zoser at Saqqara in Egypt, embedded into a wall with a capital shaped like a papyrus plant radiating up to receive masonry, is copied at King's College Chapel, Cambridge where similar columns support the fan-vaulted ceiling. The ambulatory, a partial roof supported by a portico of columns around a structural wall (usually in a courtyard), introduced the colonnade, a structure frequently used in Western architecture to this day. Examples can be seen at the Temple of Freemasonry Rite (fig. 5, p.11) and the Lincoln Memorial, both in Washington, DC.

The Greeks used Egyptian ideas and techniques and often gave them Hellenic names. Typically, the Egyptian Mammisa dispensing temple, a small raised structure with columns and an inner sanctum, became the Greek *Kiosk* used on the Erechtheion temple at the Acropolis in Athens, especially on the Caryatid Porch (see p.10), and eventually became the English pavilion. Today, we know kiosks as small shops or dispensaries. The extent of architectural development by the Greeks is limited, since the major building components in Greek architecture, the beam and column, had already been invented by the Egyptians. The pylon entrance structure allowed access into the Egyptian necropolis and was incorporated into Greek architecture as the Propylaea. Where the Greeks did make a contribution was to introduce mathematical proportions to construction that we admire and can still relate to today.

Fig. 8.

Mausoleum, London

This Mausoleum, with its mysterious and foreboding stone exterior, is clearly designed to deter the inquisitive visitor from entering. The reference to funereal architecture has its roots in the Mastaba tomb, which inspired structures such as the Cenotaph at Whitehall in London.

Fig. 9.

Mausoleum, Joensuu, 1911, Eliel Saarinen

The mausoleum is a powerful statement used to mark the final resting-place of a once-influential person, now interned without fear of being disturbed. Many elaborate designs and resources have been deployed in the construction of these structures, to ensure their continued existence and re-enforced significance.

A fine example of monumental masonry, this mausoleum in Joensuu, Finland, reflects profound loss and peace with considered reflection. The usual motifs of a mausoleum are present, including the recessed opening to the tomb structure that addresses the enclosed space within – an inviolate space, and the domain of the dead.

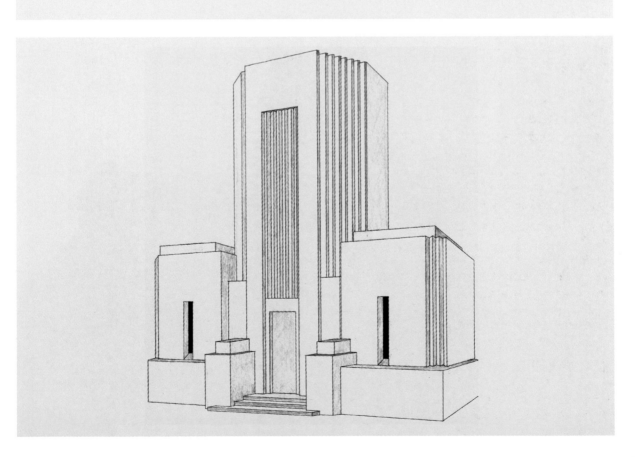

CHAPTER 2

From Fonthill Abbey to the St Pancras Hotel:
New materials and innovation

❀ The Revival of Gothic: architecture of the sublime

Gothic was originally developed in Northern Europe during the Middle Ages as an architectural style for religious buildings. The style emerged from the earlier Romanesque, the architecture of the successors of the Roman Empire and the Normans in France. In particular, the style made innovative use of the arch, incorporated to create openings in walls so as to form windows and thus allow light to flow around the structure. Abbot Suger (c.1081–1151), who oversaw construction of the Abbey of St Denis near Paris, often considered the earliest building in the Gothic style, wrote of how the new style incorporated light, which would enhance the religious experience. The style remained important for several centuries in Northern Europe.

By the 17th century, however, the Gothic style had long been overtaken by influences from the Renaissance South, and by the 18th century many Gothic buildings were no more than ruins, especially those condemned to centuries of neglect following the dissolution of the monasteries in the mid-16th century under the English king, Henry VIII. The attraction of the Gothic style in this period was its association with the 'sublime' and 'picturesque'. Without doubt Gothic buildings were very beautiful structures with ornate features, and tracery. Ruined Gothic buildings, in particular, were irregular, large dark structures with endless passages, which had a shadowy, twilight existence and offered a place where the movement of persons might take place unobserved. These evocative places seemed to symbolise the wildness of spirit typical of the emerging Romantic Movement.

At the same time an appreciation of ruins emerged as a result of the Grand Tour undertaken by the aristocracy, and by authors, artists, architects and the emerging nouveau riches during the late 18th century. The Grand Tour principally focused on the glories of Ancient Greek and Roman classical ruins, or simply a study of those ruins in the architectural drawings by Piranesi. In Britain, this led to the resurgence of interest in Gothic buildings as an indigenous Christian architecture, rather than the classical styles imported into Western Europe by the Romans from pagan Greece. In this new appreciation of the ideal of Gothic buildings, ruined or intact, was set those authors' highly charged literature involving the 'sublime' and the 'picturesque', which frequently surrounded such melancholic Gothic ruins. The literary works of Walter Scott (1771–1832), Mary Shelley (1797–1851) and William Beckford (1760–1844), for instance, often drew their inspiration from Gothic castles and ruined abbeys.

This literary response to the architecture of the ruin, especially Gothic ruins, precipitated an interest in the ideals and concepts of Gothic architecture. Those same people who had made the Grand Tour, aristocrats and nouveau riches, began to imitate the Gothic style in their own houses and in so doing created a 'Gothick' style which was principally one of adornment of existing structures.

In the mid-18th century this new 'Gothick' movement, as it was generally known, was not yet considered a serious architectural style, rather an amusing exercise in the adornment of the villas of aristocrats and emerging wealthy professionals. A primary obsession of supporters was to Gothicise any building within their control and to fund the creation of Gothick fantasies, including purpose-built ruins and follies on their country estates. Among the details of the Gothick style were turrets, battlements and tracery – raised designs usually adorning surfaces such as external walls or ceilings.

In the late 17th and early 18th centuries, during the Age of Enlightenment, Gothic architecture was considered to be retrogressive, concerned with a bygone age of medieval structures. The style was considered useful only for extending existing Gothic collegiate buildings and ecclesiastical edifices – such as in the cases of restoration work on Salisbury Cathedral by James Wyatt and Wren's work on Westminster Abbey – rather than embracing progressive, then-current ideas. However, the style attracted the attention of some notable supporters, who raised its profile, including the author and politician Horace Walpole (1717–97), son of Sir Robert Walpole, England's first Prime Minister; the architect Robert Adam (1728–92); and the wealthy philanthropist William Beckford (1760–1844).

Walpole was especially instrumental in reviving interest in the Gothic. In 1753, with the help of Robert Adam, he extended and refurbished a villa in London, turning it into a Gothick mansion. This building was later to become famous as Strawberry Hill, the architectural exercise in which Gothick-Romantic fantasy metaphors were first applied. The house had turrets, battlements, a tower and intricate tracery and patterns surrounding four-leafed quatrefoil windows and door openings set deeply

into the façade of the building. Strawberry Hill was a successful application of the Gothick style, Indeed such was its notoriety that it became a tourist destination, which prompted Walpole to publish a guidebook in 1774 for the enlightenment of visitors. Architecturally, the building inspired wealthy patrons and their architects in the construction of a series of Gothick fantasy structures across England in the mid-18th century. Notable examples are Arbury Hall in Warwickshire, adapted in the manner of Strawberry Hill into a Gothic building in the second half of the eighteenth century, and Ashridge Park in Hertfordshire, built in 1803–17 by Sir James Wyatt (1746–1813).

❀ Fonthill Abbey: a spectacular fantasy

Wyatt would become infamous for his application of the Gothick fantasy style on a super-monumental scale at the semi-ruin of the ill-fated Fonthill Abbey. The abbey was remarkable because, for the first time, Gothick design details were applied to a structure literally the size of a cathedral. This was not a house the size of Strawberry Hill or Ashridge, but the largest reconstructed fantasy in the world.

Having completed his European Grand Tour, Wyatt started out as a classical architect and applied his studies of ancient Roman ruins to designing the Pantheon in London's Oxford Street, completed in 1772. The building's dimensions were large and based on the cathedral of St Sophia at Constantinople, with a huge a circular rotunda supporting a dome. The Pantheon was effectively a pleasure parlour but it began to decline in popularity pretty soon after it opened and, by the time the initial building burnt to the ground in 1792, it had been converted into an opera house. The subsequent replacement building was also designed by Wyatt, but it was never a successful venue thereafter, although it stood until its demolition in 1937. Horace Walpole, the initiator of the

Fig. 10.
Fonthill Abbey, Wiltshire,
1796–1807, James Wyatt

A Gothick fantasy built for the psychotic
millionaire William Beckford, Fonthill
Abbey was based on Salisbury Cathedral
in England.

Gothick style at Strawberry Hill, considered the Pantheon to be the most beautiful in England. Wyatt remained a classical architect until Walpole persuaded his friend Thomas Barrett to engage Wyatt, in the years between 1785 and 1790, to Gothicise his country house at Lee Priory in Kent. Wyatt was also engaged by the wealthy and eccentric author William Beckford to turn his original building at Fonthill Abbey into the largest monumental residential Gothick fantasy in the world. This megalomaniacal project took the form of a full-size replica of Salisbury Cathedral in England, on which Wyatt had done restoration work, but with the style and dimensions of the building exaggerated to terrifying proportions in order to create the fantasy.

The reconstruction and extension of Fonthill Abbey commenced in 1796. The original building, the remnants of a Cistercian abbey, was a typical Gothic ruin. Over a period of twelve years Beckford converted it into his country retreat. However, he was a man of impatient temperament, especially with regard to this building project, the construction plans of which he inconsistently amended or revised. To speed up construction work he arranged to have huge bonfires lit to enable the workmen to build the abbey by their light during the freezing winter nights. He also managed to poach other labourers from the work going on at Windsor Castle, which was also in the process of being 'Gothicised' through the addition of new state apartments for the English king George III (1738–1820).

Although trained in classical architecture, Wyatt applied the knowledge of Gothic designs he had learnt whilst doing restoration work on Salisbury Cathedral, Westminster Abbey and King's College, Cambridge. Everything about the emerging building at Fonthill was gigantic: the main hall was 244m (800ft) long and 36.5m (120ft) high. Moreover, it was intersected in the middle by the huge 82m (270ft) high octagonal tower, which probably contributed to the building's inherent instability. Enclosed behind a 13km (8 mile) long by 3.6m (12ft) high perimeter stone wall, only the fantastic tower rising above the abbey in the centre of this walled enclosure could be seen from a distance. Inevitably, due to its rushed construction, only 18 years after completion the entire tower collapsed during one dramatic autumnal night in 1825, destroying the abbey beneath it in the process. Thus the abbey reverted back to its former state of ruin.

An account (written before the collapse) survives from one John Farquhar, employed as the Clerk of the Works during the construction of Fonthill. He admits that the foundations did not meet the specified standards and were thus defective. His only surprise was that the building was still erect. The appropriate way to describe Fonthill Abbey is by using romanticised ecclesiastical terminology to name many of the new sections: the Oratory, the Sanctuary, the Funereal Chapel, St Anthony's Altar, the Great Western Hall, St Edward's Gallery and the Crimson Breakfast Room.

Another building by Wyatt based on the same principles and building style is to be found at Ashridge Park in Hertfordshire. Ashridge is important because it affords an experience of what Fonthill Abbey might have been had it survived. It was built in the years 1803–17 as an extensive Gothick residence for the Duke of Bridgewater. However, Wyatt died in 1813 as a result of injuries sustained when his horsedrawn carriage rolled over, and the house was subsequently finished by Sir Jeffry Wyattville. Certainly the rich Gothick detailing in the stonework and on the walls, complete with opulent finishes, give this house a palatial splendour. The fan-vaulted ceiling of the private chapel approaches in magnificence the ceiling at King's College, Cambridge. Ashridge Park is one of the best-preserved Gothick residences in England.

❧ Developments in construction: the pitfalls of innovation

Just as we may feel uneasy about a building that appears at odds with its purpose, so we hesitate to embrace change in design, function and construction. For instance, despite the obvious advantages and convenience of the Otis safety elevator, it was many years before the widely held fear of the cable breaking was laid to rest. Constructing buildings using new designs with new methods and materials may at first invoke alarm at the innovation amongst the uninitiated. There are examples of bridges constructed by Brunel where the workmen refused to remove the centring timber beams upon which the brick arches were constructed lest the arches fall down. There is an innate reluctance to accept novel solutions to construction problems. This is partly because construction theory is based on trial and error, and because sometimes the results can be catastrophic, as at Fonthill Abbey.

The same fate befell Beauvais Cathedral in France, whose creation marks the zenith of adventure in Gothic architecture. Construction of the cathedral began in 1247 and continued until 1568. The builders went to great lengths to construct the highest roof in Europe, 48m (157ft), above the nave, but this collapsed catastrophically in 1284. Next came the choir section of the cathedral. This had been severely compromised by the previous collapse and was thus reconstructed with new piers in 1337. This remedial work, however, did not prevent the huge 500ft-high tower from collapsing catastrophically in 1573. Other minor problems and failures had occurred throughout the course of the cathedral's prolonged construction. This project demonstrates, apart from the admirable quality of perseverance, the adage that one should not correct one mistake with a further mistake. The basic structure at Beauvais was inherently unsound and liable to intermittent failure! Rather than demolish what was left of the cathedral and build a new one, the builders merely amended the present structure, thus failing to learn from their mistakes. Unlike Fonthill Abbey, a similar structure, which took 12 years to build before collapsing a further 18 years later, Beauvais Cathedral was built slowly over more than three centuries – with all the time for sober reflection that would suggest – yet still kept falling down. Luckily, the mishaps at Fonthill and Beauvais are very much the exception, new structures are constructed and eventually accepted as part of the built environment, in part because the designs of most buildings, despite their apparent novelty, are in fact based on tried and endlessly tested structural principles.

❧ Neo-Gothic: Victorian extravagance

Despite the troubled history of Fonthill Abbey, the Gothick movement was widely influential across England, and replaced the previously popular Neoclassical style that characterised state and much residential architecture of the 18th century. The Neoclassical style was based upon classical ideals so as to produce an understated elegance. However, buildings were restrained on account of structural considerations, which could affect the amount of daylight that reached the interior.

By contrast, the Victorian 'Gothic Revival' style, also known as Neo-Gothic (an eminent example of which can be seen in the St Pancras Hotel in London – see figs 12 and 18), was generally out to make a statement, complete with ornamentation. The style was a continuation of the Gothick Movement of the 18th century, but the Victorians developed building methods using new materials such as glass in vast expanses and iron, and in doing so created structures where daylight could penetrate. A famous example was the new Palace of Westminster in London (mostly completed by 1860), which stretched the Gothic idiom to remarkable proportions. The idea here was to impress the observer, and its being sited on the Thames Embankment afforded an uninterrupted view from the opposite bank of the river, by which its presence and importance could be fully appreciated.

New developments: the rise of the engineer

In the 18th century a new titan appeared in the field of construction, the professional civil engineer. The rise of the civil, as opposed to military, engineer was a result of advancements made during a series of industrial revolutions, particularly in England. This new profession dedicated itself to the appreciation of mechanical and structural ideas and the application of Newton's Laws of Motion. It ushered in the great period of technology-based approaches to construction (which still continues to this day), typified in the works of Isambard Kingdom Brunel (1806–59), Robert Stephenson (1803–59) and Thomas Telford (1757–1834). A new scientific understanding of materials, such as iron and later steel, was also increasingly applied to construction projects.

In the same period, there were also significant advancements in the production of such materials, leading to a massive expansion in building programmes throughout the Western world. Without these new materials there would have been very little innovative construction that did not conform to the limitations of previous building methods and architectural styles.

The hydraulic engine: power and precision

Early Victorian engineers continued this development of materials: iron for bridges; Portland cement-based concrete for dams and harbours; ceramic tiles and rustproof metal alloys (of zinc, tin, copper, brass and mild steel) for steam and hydraulic engines. The Victorians were fascinated by machinery that could be used to create the new forms of power needed to realise their ambitious construction projects, which would previously have been unachievable without huge armies of labour on a scale comparable with the workforce that built the Pyramids. One machine in particular that focused the Victorian mind, because of its potential to release controlled power, was the hydraulic engine. Its applications were as immense as they were varied. Telford used hydraulic engines to position the main iron girders on his bridge over the Menai Strait between mainland Wales and the island of Anglesey, which was opened in 1826. In 1858 Brunel used hydraulic engines to launch his prototype iron ship, the *SS Great Eastern*, into the River Thames in London. The hydraulic engine could deliver a great force in one direction and was deployed typically to manoeuvre massive inert objects weighing several tons into an exact position.

The concept of the hydraulic engine is a simple one. It involves pumping a fluid, usually oil under pressure, into a primary piston chamber. That fluid is then compressed into a secondary larger chamber. The difference in chamber sizes produces two distinct forces, the *mechanical advantage* and the *velocity ratio*.

The *mechanical advantage* is the effort, measured in tons, required to move the primary piston, which will be considerably less than the resultant force exerted by the secondary piston. In effect, effort expressed as 10 tons could lift a weight of 50 tons.

In so doing, the other force, *velocity ratio*, becomes applicable. This is the length along which that force travels, represented by the secondary piston. For example, the primary piston may move five metres as *effort* while pushing the secondary piston as *result* a distance of only one metre.

Invariably moving heavy objects consumes energy and is a slow process. Despite this, the hydraulic engine enabled the engineer to control this prodigious power, using it to position massive inert objects precisely in place. For example, an iron girder weighing several tons could be located, albeit slowly, onto a vertical pier in the construction of a bridge, as was the case with Telford's Menai Bridge. Masonry blocks could be manoeuvred in the formation of dams, tunnels, viaducts, harbour walls, railroads and buildings, all of which were crucial in creating the infrastructure of a developing industrial nation.

The use of the hydraulic engine and its role in Victorian construction was as crucial to Victorian engineering and construction as the tower crane is to the builder today. The hydraulic engine was particularly instrumental in the evolution of the elevator for use in tall buildings, and therefore in the development of the skyscraper (see Chapter 6). The original Equitable Building in New York, completed in 1870 and considered by some to be the world's first skyscraper, used Otis elevators powered by hydraulic engines.

✵ New professions: expansion of the construction industry

The availability of new materials and technology during the 19th century allowed rapid development in construction and engineering, creating a gap between earlier building methods, carried out by architects, and new ideas, promoted by engineers. New professions emerged in construction alongside the civil engineer, including the structural engineer and surveyor. This development produced an interesting shift in the understanding of the design of structures, which had far-reaching implications for architecture, engineering and the construction process, which came to involve other disciplines such as economics and the arts.

✵ Does function follow form or does form follow function?

Similar to the concept 'is a glass half empty or half full?', there is no right or wrong answer as to whether form should follow function or vice

versa, but the question itself offers a fascinating way of viewing structures. It is also useful to think beyond what is immediately visible before assessing reality.

Does function follow form – hiding the infrastructure? In the past, architects were very likely to hide certain functions or disguise them with covering finishes. Typical of this approach is a ventilation shaft to draw car exhaust fumes away from the Mersey Road Tunnel in Liverpool, opened in 1934. The architect Herbert Rowse (1887–1963) made the shaft tower 30.5m (100ft) high and encased it in an elaborate Art Deco façade. This Art Deco cladding effectively hides the function of the shaft so that it more closely resembles a dignified public building than a utilitarian chimney. The required function of the shaft – ventilation – follows the form of a structure designed to imitate a building. The function of the chimney is subordinate to its physical features.

Does form follow function – exposing the infrastructure? To the engineer this makes good sense; why hide the structure with covering finishes? The George Washington Bridge in New York is a good example. This huge double-decked suspension bridge is supported by steel cables from two 183m (600ft) high steel towers, and was built to link Washington Heights in Manhattan to Fort Lee in New Jersey across the Hudson River. There is not one square inch of decorative finish applied to its exposed steel piers, girders and transoms.

But the concept can also be reversed – for example, when considering the construction by Sir Joseph Paxton (1801–65) and Gustav Eiffel (1832–1923) of Victorian exhibition halls, which were built usually of an exposed iron frame and glass windows. Here an exception to the rule could apply, putting the concept into reverse. One might admire an exhibition hall of iron and glass for its own sake, *function follows form*, as could have been the case at the Crystal Palace (1851) by Joseph Paxton, more than for what

Fig. 11.

Mausoleum-style structure,
Canary Wharf, London, 1989,
Skidmore, Owings and Merrill.

This contemporary structure is located
on the approaches to the main tower
at Canary Wharf, London. Its purpose
is to conceal a ventilation shaft, but its
design was greatly influenced by funereal
architecture. The meticulous metallic
decoration and finishes to the exterior
are in the style of design details typical
of the 1920s and 1930s.

the building was built to exhibit, *form follows function*. We may have forgotten what was being *exhibited in* the Crystal Palace but we do remember what the building looked like. So which came first in this case: *function following form or form following function?*

❀ North American railroads and railways in Great Britain: functional solutions

After the American Civil War, US industry and commerce settled down to recover business and continue progress and expansion west across the continent to the Pacific. Emphasis was placed on moving people and materials in order to accomplish these aims. During this great building period of the 19th century, concerns about aesthetic beauty in construction were less important than in an established country like England. The majority of railroad bridges built in America were of the cheap trestle type, made out of timber. In England bridges were invariably made of dressed stone, or else magnificent stone and iron structures as Telford's Menai Strait Bridge. The alternatives deployed in America were cheaper because the emphasis was on settling and developing a huge continental landmass, and the cheaper and quicker to build the transport systems the easier it would be in the short term to move goods, people and raw materials from one region to another. For this reason, architectural solutions tended to be more functional in the United States.

When the first railways into London were built, most were at ground level or in deep cuttings. Throughout the 19th century, railway promoters seeking permission from Parliament to construct new railways spent time and energy battling aristocratic landlords who refused to allow railway lines to cross their estates. Brunel, when constructing the Great Western Railway to Bristol, was compelled to build the two-mile-long Box Tunnel, lined with 30 million bricks and announced by a very ornate stone entrance at the western end, so as to placate a local landowner who did not want sight of the train.

This approach was repeated for the first underground railways in mid-Victorian London. The District line in the south and Metropolitan line in the north were the first subterranean London railway lines, and were submerged into a canyon cut into the ground and then covered with the newly constructed Thames Embankment Road and the Euston and Marylebone Roads respectively, which even today effectively hide the operation of the railway. As these lines radiated out from the city into the suburbs, they were laid at ground level. The London underground system, known as the Tube, was inaugurated with the opening in 1890 of the City and South London Railway (now part of the Northern line) as this offered the most economical way of providing an urban railway system using bored tunnels.

❀ Exhibition halls: iron and glass

Victorian engineers rarely applied covering finishes to a structure, preferring instead to let form follow function. A good example came at the Great Exhibition in London of 1851. It pioneered the use of pre-fabricated buildings of iron and glass that were capable of being erected on site in a matter of weeks rather than months. The Crystal Palace is a famous example of this approach to construction, in which an exposed iron frame is covered with glass panels. Following the Great Exhibition two similar structures were erected in Britain: a temporary structure, modelled on the Crystal Palace, was built in Manchester in 1857 to house the Art Treasures Exhibition attended by Queen Victoria; and in 1862, a conservatory was built by the Royal Horticultural Society at South Kensington in London.

Victorian engineers were the great exponents of iron-framed glazed conservatories and exhibition halls, which allowed the creation of spaces illuminated solely by daylight. However, in the main these structures were allowed to exist only for a limited period – say, the duration of an exhibition. Some, however, have remained, belying that sense of impermanence – structures such as Alexandra Palace, or the Olympia and Earl's Court exhibition halls in London; others, like the Crystal Palace, were removed to another location. The reason these structures were perceived as temporary was due to their style of construction; made from an exposed iron frame with glass panes, they were not properly covered in an acceptable, lasting finish such as stone, brick or timber. Consequently, most 19th-century exhibition halls were dismantled – aside from the Crystal Palace (which was reassembled before being burned to the ground in 1936), similar buildings at the Paris Exposition of 1878 and the Paris Exposition Universelle of 1889 were also not to last. In addition to the building housing the Art Treasures Exhibition building in Manchester, in 1857, and the Exhibition Building of 1862 in London, the extensive International Exhibition building in Glasgow in 1888 was also pulled down after only a matter of months.

❄ New methods in construction: fast iron frames

Concepts in construction process, mass production, and use of the iron frame that had been learned in the 18th century affected the course and direction of building in the 19th century. Major construction projects were begun that remain the basis of our understanding of construction methods. The first iron bridge, designed by Abraham Derby, was built at Coalbrookdale in Shropshire in 1779. Cast iron was used increasingly for structural purposes in the form of columns and girders for the construction of mills, which were needed for the mass production of goods. During the 18th century's final decade William Strutt built several mills in Derbyshire using iron. As the need for manufacturing premises grew unabated so did the need for transport infrastructure to service those factories. This necessitated the construction of railways, canals, dams and roads throughout Britain and later in the United States and around the world. At the same time, the British Parliament established funds for the provision of public buildings including workhouses, churches, schools and museums. In response, various types of buildings were created that deviated from the previous stricture that buildings should conform to the style of the age – Elizabethan, Jacobean, Georgian, etc. The Victorians were innovators in the sense that they were not so concerned with the development of a distinctive style but with the application of construction concepts.

The Victorians reaped the results, beneficial or not, of early industrialisation in England. The series of earlier industrial revolutions ensured that a new *modus operandi* would be imposed on the design of buildings. This new understanding of society, in which the general good of society is best served by the operation of the free market, was clearly propounded by Adam Smith (1723–90) in his seminal text *The Wealth of Nations*, written in 1776. The innovations in science and in industrial production had the effect of accelerating the development of technology, which was being yoked to the task of creating wealth rather than aesthetic structures. There was, in effect, a mini gold rush, in which cheap buildings were put up to house the new factories. In this respect, the Victorians were innovators concerned with the application of construction process concepts, mass production and the iron frame, rather than design. This may account for why they failed to invent their own distinctive style of architecture, instead falling back on a series of 'revival' styles – for example, adopting the Gothick design traits of the mid-18th century, which later became the Gothic Revival of the 1830s onwards. The revival of the style was, in part, due to its appealing, familiar form and enduring Romantic image.

Where the Victorians did not use Gothic or Classical designs they merely deferred to the Queen Anne style. This style was considered suitable because it was dignified and cheap to realise. It was adopted, for example, by the London Board Schools during the 1870s by architect E. R. Robson (1835–1917), notably at West Street School at London Fields. The fabric of buildings in this style was of brickwork, and it was ornamented with stone dressing to the corners, pedimented window reveals and doorways, typical of Norman Shaw (1831–1912) at Lowther Lodge (built in 1874) and 170 Queensgate (built in 1888), both in Kensington, London.

Leading this progress in innovation with materials was iron, a material of the utmost versatility, which began to be produced industrially from about 1750. Iron girders were able to accept levels of structural tension that masonry and timber beams simply could not. Obvious applications of this metal can be seen in the construction of railway stations, coastal piers, bandstands, railings and arcades throughout the Victorian period. Iron sections could be fabricated off site in a foundry and assembled on site to construct a building. This is how the Crystal Palace in London was built in a matter of weeks in 1851 and similarly Paddington railway station, also in London, in 1854. Indeed ballrooms, warehouses and clock towers made of iron could be prefabricated and shipped aboard.

An adaptation of this method of construction, the exposed iron frame with glass windows, facilitated another Victorian innovation, that of the iron-framed, or cage, building. This frame received the load-bearing forces of the building and removed the need for heavy masonry, instead allowing construction of lighter external walls and spanning larger voids within the building to create uncluttered space.

Two major trends emerged in construction based on the iron frame. The first was a construction method that maximised available space for the minimum investment – a cheap building. Typically, the construction of a factory would involve the use of cast-iron columns supporting cast-iron cross beams upon which were set timber-decked floors. This allowed the factory owner the maximum space to devote to machinery and workforce. The building would be clad in low-cost brick, while large glazed areas provided natural light, avoiding the need for expensive artificial lighting.

The second trend was for impressive stone-clad buildings – commercial offices, private residences, railway stations, universities and government buildings – built using technological advances in iron manufacture to create a metal superstructure, on which the expensive ornamentation could be fixed. It was easier, cheaper and more practical to hide a metal-framed structure within a Victorian Neo-Gothic design than to fund the creation of an authentic Gothic building, complete with the traditional forest of solid stone columns, flying buttresses with pinnacles and groin vaulting, which would compromise the intended contemporary use of the building. An exception, however, was the Royal Courts of Justice in London, designed by G.E. Street and opened in 1882. Street advocated the authentic traditional Gothic methods of construction, and the iron frame was dispensed with as the architect's intention was to create a modern Gothic building of cathedral proportions.

A further development involved iron being used in conjunction with the new improved Portland cement. Here iron girders were embedded in the cement, creating a reinforced beam capable of coping with the immense compressive and tensile forces that arise in a large structure. This innovation was used in the construction in 1867 of the Neo-Gothic St Pancras Hotel in London (pp.47–9), which fronted the St Pancras Railway station, the terminus of the London Midland Railway. Iron was also used in fabricating the metal and glass roof over the adjoining railway-station platforms, just as it had been for the roof at Paddington station in the early 1850s. This Victorian metal-frame concept was used later by William LeBaron Jenney (1832–1907)

Fig. 12.
St Pancras Hotel, London, 1867,
George Gilbert Scott

Designed as the prototype for the Foreign
Office in 1867, this became the terminus
for the London Midland Railway. The
mannerism of the building reflects
the High Victorian Gothic style current
at the time. The Victorians built their
Neo-Gothic structures inexpensively
and quickly using the new iron frame
technology.

in the development and construction of the first skyscrapers in Chicago in the 1880s.

The Victorians were seen as being inventive and enjoying the prosperity that came with political stability and the resources of a large empire. Ultimately it was the iron-framed Neo-Gothic style of the St Pancras Hotel, the High Victorian secular Gothic, which became the dominant architectural style.

The St Pancras Hotel is not just a hotel that happens to be built in the Gothic style. Rather it represents a victory in the battle of architectural styles that had raged since 1836, with the Gothic style, for instance, being selected for the new Palace of Westminster in London. Despite that decision, classical buildings were still being constructed – notably St George's Hall in Liverpool (1840–54), the Fitzwilliam Museum in Cambridge, England (1837–47) and the Foreign Office in London's Whitehall (1860–75). The St Pancras Hotel was pivotal in the evolution and acceptance of the Neo-Gothic style in England based on the iron frame. The Victorians adopted this technique enthusiastically, applying iron-frame technology to construct, quickly and cheaply, decorative pseudo-Gothic buildings throughout Britain and its Empire – notably, the Dominion Parliament Buildings at Ottawa (1861–67), designed by Thomas Fuller (1823–98), and F.W. Stevens's Victoria Terminus in Bombay (now the Chhatrapati Shivaji Terminus in Mumbai) in India (opened in 1887). This station was built to be as substantial in size as the St Pancras Hotel and St Pancras Station in London, to which it bears some resemblance. Both the Parliament Buildings and the Victoria Terminus are obvious statements of the Victorian conviction that the soaring Neo-Gothic style could convey their values and importance overseas.

❧ Interior design: fittings and furnishings

While falling back on historical styles in their architecture, the Victorians did create their own extravagant and exuberant urban vernacular interior design. This was especially true in theatres and public houses, which combined a fantasy of Queen Anne or Baroque-styled interiors. Such interiors were usually fitted with highly polished mahogany woodwork with brass fittings, handrails and gas globe lanterns, as well as rich velvet drapes of red, green or purple that framed engraved windows and decorative glazed openings in the internal partitioning walls. Painted moulded-plaster ceilings and elaborately patterned carpets, complete with ubiquitous indoor palm trees, were designed to inveigle customers and patrons into these opulent establishments. This plush approach to interior design is what most people nowadays associate with the Victorian style. It was emulated in a more sedate manner in the edifices of the late Victorian period: hotels, gentlemen's clubs, museums, art galleries and commercial offices, and the parlours of town and country houses – all were adorned in this popular Victorian style.

The Victorians would plush up their interiors as a reaction to the rough exterior that was the perceived outside world. Heavy velvet drapes were deployed over windows and doors to check the ability of the outside world to encroach upon the Victorian interior. Notable examples of Victorian interiors in London can be found at the Criterion Bar in Piccadilly, the Paxton's Head in Knightsbridge, the Lord Salisbury public house and the Charing Cross Hotel both at Charing Cross. Finally, the Rising Sun in London's Fitzrovia (built in 1896), with its window openings carved deeply into highly decorated exterior walls, shows clearly that despite the Victorians' industrial might and brave innovative spirit, they still retained in their hearts a deep fondness for the Gothick style.

Spiritual crisis:
a retreat into fantasy

As the needs of a rapidly growing population increased, so did their requirement for more buildings. However, the Victorians for all their progress and success were deeply troubled by the concept of death. Scientific advances, especially Darwin's theory of natural selection and the work of Thomas Huxley, suggested the improbability of God and questioned the relevance of scripture, which subsequently led to the Church's authority and its ability to guarantee peaceful repose after death being challenged. The Victorians sought a refuge and consolation in fantasy and in symbolism, to replace the old regime of belief. This embracing of spiritualism can be seen in the work of contemporary artists, writers and musicians. Members of the Pre-Raphaelite Brotherhood, including Dante Gabriel Rossetti, John Everett Millais and Edward Burne-Jones, concerned themselves with subjects from literature and poetry dealing with love and death, and scenes of chivalry and romance; themes based on the Arthurian legend were particularly popular.

However, the psychological instability of the Pre-Raphaelite Movement betrayed a sense of unease within Victorian society more generally. A case in point was the painter and poet Rossetti's reaction to the death of his wife, Elizabeth Siddal. She modelled for most of the Pre-Raphaelite artists at the time and was later immortalised in her portrait *Astarte Syriaca* (1877). Elizabeth died of an overdose of laudanum in 1862, at a time when Victorian anxieties about death were at an extreme. Rossetti was overcome with grief and could not quite bring himself to accept her death, insisting that her corpse be left exposed for seven days in the vain hope she might recover. She did not, and was eventually buried in a mausoleum in the Egyptian Avenue in the Western Cemetery at Highgate in London. However, before her coffin was bricked up in the mausoleum, Rossetti had placed in it the only existing copy of his collected poems. Seven years later when his grief had diminished, he had second thoughts and exhumed Elizabeth's coffin in order to recover the lost poems! Rossetti's maudlin fascination with death was typical of the period. An acclaimed and innovative artist in his time, Rossetti profoundly influenced the Victorian mind in its dealings with what was perceived to be the hereafter. In 1895, Millais (1829–96) painted a spiritual scene, *Speak! Speak!*, in which a dead wife is depicted in her bridal gown at the foot of the bed, exhorting her living husband to join her!

Other artists, especially those of the Olympian trend including Frederic Leighton (1830–96), Edward Poynter (1836–1919), Lawrence Alma-Tadema (1836–1912) and G.F. Watts (1817–1904), depicted scenes of classical buildings and temples in which classical gods disported themselves in this newly perceived God-less world. The sober Atkinson Grimshaw (1836–93), on the other hand, painted melancholic moonlight and autumnal scenes, especially in Yorkshire, but often ventured into the world of reveries and fairies – for instance, the nymph fluttering above the lake in his painting *Iris* (1886). Charles Doyle, father of Sir Arthur Conan Doyle (author of the Sherlock Holmes stories), who also believed vehemently in spirits, was another renowned painter of scenes depicting preoccupied fairies. The theme was taken up in painting by Francis Danby's *Wood Nymph* and in David Scott's the *Enchanted Island*. This pervasive Victorian yearning for a romantic escape from reality to oblivion and fantasy was also represented in music, notably in the operas of Richard Wagner (1813–83) such as *Die Feen* (*The Fairies*). (This trend continued into the Edwardian era in works by the Master of the Queen's Music, Sir Edward Elgar.) This combined artistic output from artists, writers and musicians not only satisfied a deep public appetite for fantasy and escapism but had the effect of perpetuating it.

Fantasy and fairies played a prominent role in the Victorian mind, a symptom of a wish to retreat into Romantic oblivion. Fantasy was generally accepted and tolerated and was promoted by a range of artists in the late Victorian period. It may at first seem incongruous to conceive the idea that perhaps fantasy may have been the inspiration behind the designs of huge railway stations, but it was. Notable buildings of the period were clearly fantasy creations, among them William Burges's renovated Cardiff Castle, and the St Pancras Hotel.

Outside of the UK, the use of fantasy in architecture was taken to its ultimate conclusion in the Romantic castles built by the insane Ludwig II, King of Bavaria (1845–86). The designs for his castles were based on scenes straight out of Wagnerian opera. The most famous example is the castle of Neuschwanstein, which was built on the top of a Bavarian mountain between 1869 and 1886, complete with stretched pinnacles, turrets and towers. ⚜

❈ Neo-Gothic in the United States: the Gothic Water Tower

Gothic architecture was never a universally accepted idiom in the United States, where architects were increasingly keen to forge a distinctly American idiom. Certainly in the 18th century classical architecture was the Establishment style, especially on the British-influenced Atlantic seaboard. Montecello House (1770–1808) in Virginia and the White House (1792–1800) in Washington, DC, are considered products of a classically based architecture of logic rather than religious zeal and decoration. Elsewhere in the emerging United States other European styles were being applied, from French Second Emprie style in the Louisiana region and towards Canada, to Spanish in the Southwest. There are some Neo-Gothic structures in the United States but they tend to be collegiate buildings. Some railroad stations, as in Richard Montfort's and H.H. Richardson's Union Station (1900) in Nashville, Tennessee, are dressed in Gothic designs below a statue of Mercury representing the very modern railroad. The Union Pacific Railroad Station (1891–94) at St Louis, Missouri, by Theodore Link (1850–1923), addressed a fantasy of Gothic but from a Romanesque perspective, creating what in 1894 was the largest railroad station in the world.

The Gothic Water Tower of 1869 by architect William W. Boyington, in central Chicago on North Michigan Avenue is a notable example of the American Neo-Gothic. Built to house a 46m (150ft) high standpipe, needed to equalize the pressure of water pumped from a pumping station in the east of metropolitan Chicago, its practical function was not reflected in its Romantic decoration. It is quite clearly a Gothic fantasy tower, complete with battlements, turrets and tracery to its walls. Being constructed using an iron frame and clad in Illinois limestone gave it protection during the Great Chicago Fire of 1871; that it survived led people toward favouring iron-framed buildings in the form of skyscrapers. Notwithstanding the building's practical functionalty, the Romanticsm inherent in the design of the Water Tower pales into insignificance when considered in relation to the Romantic structures being built in Europe, notably in Bavaria.

Fig. 13.

Gothic Water Tower, Chicago, 1869, William W. Boynington

The Tower was designed in 1869 as a practical solution to the problem of equalising the piped water pressure in central Chicago. Made from an iron frame clad in Illinois limestone blocks, it survived the Great Chicago Fire which engulfed and destroyed the city in 1871. As a result of the fire all buildings in metropolitan Chicago constructed after 1871 had to be built using fire retardant materials, including stone and iron, in order to prevent a repeat of the disaster. The iron frame construction of the Tower pioneered the way for the evolution of the first iron framed fire-proof skyscrapers, the design of which were to dominate American construction systems for the next fourteen decades. Once again, a fantasy-style building evolved into a method of designing and constructing huge structures – skyscrapers – that dominate our modern-day cities.

CHAPTER 3

The largest room in the world: building to impress

🌸 Architecture for identity: confident corporations

In an attempt to make their existence known to the public, railroad corporations, commercial companies, churches and government bodies create buildings that are a generally recognisable and a focal point by which to be identified. The owner's purpose and in some cases wealth (and, by implication, success) was manifest in the building's mannerisms. For instance, a railroad corporation operates a series of permanent ways over a geographical region with intermediate stations and depots. One of the features that make a railroad corporation identifiable – in some cases over thousands of miles of tracks across an entire continent – is the manner of arrival at the stations, the gateways to their system. This experience is at its most compelling when arriving at a railroad's premier station. Grand Central Terminal (1903) or Pennsylvania Railroad Station (1906) both in New York, were designed in accordance with the principles of the Beaux-Arts style. As we have seen, St Pancras Station in London followed the Neo-Gothic style that was prominent in Britain during the Victorian era. All were designed to represent unequivocally the economic power and ambition of railroad corporations.

A fundamental component of these structures was the use of an iron infrastructure. Onto the iron frame could be fixed a polished stone façade with ornament, the technology supporting, quite literally, the concepts and designs of classical architecture. This facility enabled the construction of the great buildings and railroad stations of the Beaux-Arts era of the early 20th century.

🌸 Beaux-Arts

The basic building method of Beaux-Arts construction was to fix imposing carved limestone masonry blocks to a building's metal frame – creating a stone fabric that gave the impression of an edifice built entirely of stone blocks. The stone façade was decorated with ornate carvings, relief, statuary, crotches, corporation ciphers, bronze and nickel metal fixtures including window and door frames, ornamental lamps, emblems, signage and general ostentatious paraphernalia. The idea was to create an impressive building, at an affordable cost.

In general, the distinguishing feature of the interiors of Beaux-Arts buildings is the extravagant use of masonry blocks, usually of polished limestone or sandstone, to form the internal walls, floors, arches and bridges, emphasizing keystones, internal balconies, columns and stairs. These features were deployed in New York at Grand Central Terminal, Pennsylvania Railroad Station and the American Museum of Natural History. The interior structure would incorporate wide low arches that create openings into the different areas of the building. The same technique would be deployed with stone balustrades on internal bridges linking one space with another, and on broad staircases of polished limestone ascending to the upper levels, with intricate metal balustrades and ornamental bronze or limestone statues on each of the landings supporting globe lanterns that radiate electric light. Elaborate sections of cornice and architrave would cap the stonework and walls, interrupted only by pilasters and piers supporting decorative arches. The whole effect is of a lavish, powerful interior of pale-yellow warm polished stone reflecting light from dazzling bronze light globes – a successful evocation of the splendour of Imperial Rome.

On the front of Grand Central Terminal in New York this extravagant approach to decoration is evoked by the carvings in the monumental statue relief group dominated by Mercury, the Roman god of speed (and, by implication, transport), representing the railroad corporations. At Grand Central Terminal, Mercury can be seen addressing 42nd Street in all his god-like mute arrogance on the stone entablature above the main portico. At Nashville Union Station in Tennessee he adorns the top of the tower of the station. His presence speaks of the confidence of the railroad corporations of the time, as yet unchallenged by other forms of mass transportation.

The grand scale and dignity of the Beaux-Arts tradition is essentially a 19th-century application of classical architecture. It turned to various technological innovations of the time, including the use of a steel frame to receive the stone façade and ornamentation so as to re-create a classical idiom fulfilling the railroad company's desire to display commercial power. In this respect the prototype railway station in Paris, designed by Victor Laloux, Lucien Magne and Émile Bénard, the Gare D'Orsay (1900) is considered by architectural historian Carroll Meeks, 'to be a model station, destined to influence many others'. Its design and construction methods were seized upon by architects in America searching for a new medium to express their patrons' power.

In the early part of the 20th century, American corporations such as Vanderbilt, Rockefeller, Stanford, Cassatt, JP Morgan and Carnegie considered themselves in imperial terms, with vast resources and influence around the United States, if not the world. It was therefore quite fitting for them, in erecting monuments to their enduring wealth and economic power, to choose building designs in the Beaux-Arts style that clearly reflected the past splendours of Imperial Rome. This was repeated in major cities across America.

Pennsylvania Railroad Terminal: the largest room in the world

One such Titan with serious imperial ambitions was Alexander Cassatt, President of the Pennsylvania Railroad. He wanted a new station in New York for his Pennsylvania Railroad that would represent a monumental entrance to the commercial metropolis of the United States. Previously the Pennsylvania Railroad, coming in from the West, had terminated at Jersey City, New Jersey. Passengers travelling on to New York City were compelled to take the ferry across the Hudson River to Manhattan. Similarly, passengers travelling in from the East used the Long Island Railroad, a branch line of the Pennsylvania Railroad, and alighted at Long Island City, located on the eastern side of the East River. Again a ferry service conveyed passengers into New York City. Cassatt appointed the architects McKim, Mead & White to design a new station for him, in the Beaux-Arts style. These architects were instrumental in promoting Beaux-Arts in America, following its success at the Gare D'Orsay in Paris and its formal introduction into America at the World's Columbian Exposition of 1893 in Chicago.

What Cassatt had in mind was a railroad station like no other, given the property constraints in Manhattan around 34th Street on 7th and 8th Avenues, which prevented the trains travelling overland to the station. His intention was to

Fig. 14.

*Pennsylvania Railroad Station,
New York, completed 1911,
McKim, Mead and White*

This drawing shows construction in
progress of the 'largest room in the
world', which was based upon the baths
of Imperial Rome (notably the Thermae of
Caracalla). The combination of Imperial
Roman and Beaux-Arts styles resulted
in an astonishing structure, built with
polished limestone blocks complete with
extravagant designs set into stone facia
and complimented with nickel and bronze
ornamentation. The Pennsylvania Railroad
Station was demolished in the 1960s,
leaving the Grand Central Terminal as the
only functioning example of Beaux-Arts
railroad architecture in New York.

apply the adaptability and flexibility of Beaux-Arts designs, and the style's inherent embrace of technology, with American pragmatism. For one thing the train station would be submerged 14m (45ft) below ground to receive the railroad tracks coming in from newly constructed tunnels linking train services from Jersey City in the West to Long Island City in the East.

Below ground were located the functional aspects of the station. A network of massive steel piers and girders was used to allow space to be created below ground and support the superstructure of the Great Hall above. The space allowed freedom and rapid movement of goods and people within the confines of the subterranean complex, and also the installation of electrically operated machinery to power innovative equipment such as luggage conveyor systems, elevators and water pumps. One of the achievements of the design was the introduction and regular use of the new electric locomotives, thus eliminating at a stroke the serious safety, fire and health problems caused by smoke emanating from the coal-fuelled locomotives used on other railroads.

Above ground was located the Great Hall, modelled on the Imperial Roman Baths at Caracalla. Here the Beaux-Arts style was applied in all its ostentatious splendour to create 'the largest and most monumental single room in the world today'. Essentially a redundant space and therefore useful only as a concourse waiting room, in its magnificence the Great Hall nevertheless reflected the engineering marvel located below it.

Despite the architectural innovations achieved at the Pennsylvania Railroad Station it was demolished in 1963 with the connivance of Mayor Wagner of New York, who, representing the public interest, dismissed an application to have the New York Landmarks Preservation Commission intervene to save the structure from redevelopment. The reason for this was that in 1960 the railroad corporation advised

its stockholders it was making losses of $15,000,000. In order to reverse this trend the corporation published in the 21st July 1961 edition of the New York Times plans to redevelop the 'air rights' above the station to create a new Madison Square Garden entertainment complex. There was a spirited campaign to save the structure but ultimately the railroad corporation's inalienable rights to exist in a financially viable way and to develop its property held sway over public opinion, as confirmed by the Supreme Court.

The dramatic language of the Beaux-Arts was especially popular in the United States, where an technologically innovative architectural style reflecting wealth and power was keenly embraced. It was successfully used in the design of railroad stations, banks and other financial institutions, as well as monuments, mansion blocks and public buildings such as New York's American Museum of Natural History. Beaux-Arts designs were the basis of the engineering and style on the Hell Gate Bridge (begun in 1911), designed by civil engineer Gustav Lindenthal to bring the Pennsylvania Railroad over the East River into Manhattan.

The bridge comprises two massive granite-clad masonry abutments to which is anchored each end of the parabolic, a low curved-steel arch. These monumental abutments, linked by the steel arch and dressed in classical motifs expressed as cantilevered cornices, stone arches and crowning balustrades, cast a retrospective look at the classicism embodied in the ideals of the Beaux-Arts. The towers serve no structural purpose but do create the illusion that they are holding up the bridge by receiving the steel girders, whereas these are in fact anchored straight into the foundations of the masonry abutments. The real purpose of stone cladding is merely to hide the collection of structural girders supporting the elevated section of the railroad. However, in true Beaux-Arts style, the towers display a number of design features that are typical of the classical idiom. For example, the detailing on the towers

Fig. 15.

Hell Gate Railroad Bridge, New York, 1911, Gustav Lindenthal

The bridge was begun in 1911 over the East River in New York for the Pennsylvania Railroad. This structure is a retrospective look at detailing of Classicism expressed in the the structurally redundant, albeit ornate, abutments comprising deep vertical voids twenty feet wide, virtually forming two piers and which divide the parabolic suspension bridge proper from the steel viaduct carrying the elevated railroad as a fitting route for the entry into New York.

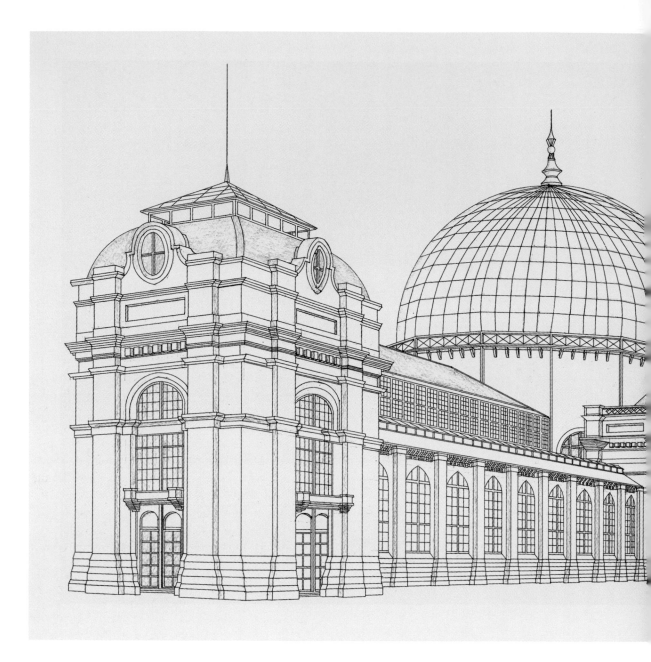

Fig. 16.
Exhibition Building, 1862,
Francis Fowke

The Exhibition Building was Fowke's attempt to
introduce Beaux-Arts architecture to England.
The attempt failed, and the building was pulled
down shortly after completion, having been
described as, 'one of the ugliest public buildings
that was ever raised in this country!' Such criticism
was unwarranted, as it displayed elements of beauty
and balance in the application in its restrained
Beaux-Arts design.

constructed using arches, creating deep vertical voids 6m (20ft) wide, forming two distinct piers in each of the masonry towers. Notice also that the masonry to the towers' upper sections is completed with cantilevered cornices supporting crowning balustrades.

In the same year the Hell Gate Bridge was designed, the firm of Warren & Whetmore were appointed as chief architects, replacing the architectural firm of Reed & Stem. The Vanderbilt family, owners of the New York Central Railroad, had called for a competition for the design of a new Grand Central Terminal at 42nd Street, New York, which Reed & Stem had duly won. However, competing nepotisms saw to it that, while Charles Reed was the brother-in-law of William Wilgus – the Chief Engineer of the New York Central Railroad – Whitney Warren's connection as a cousin of Cornelius Vanderbilt – President of the New York Central Railroad – ensured that in the end he won overall supervision of the project. Warren had studied and taught at the École des Beaux-Arts in Paris and returned home to champion Beaux-Arts architecture in America. The completed building was a successful and sympathetic interpretation of the academic ideals of Beaux-Arts designs – invoking classical grandeur but underpinned with up-to-date technology and current scientific method. An example of this grandeur took the form of an Imperial Rome-inspired triumphal arch façade entrance into the terminal, signifying a momentous arrival into the City of New York. Adjacent are Corinthian columns of limestone, sculptural groups and ornate details set into the walls. The floors and staircases are of highly polished travertine stone and Tennessee marble. Fixed to the exterior façade are carvings, gilded plasterwork, bronze or nickel metal fixtures, ornamental globe lamps, railings and ubiquitous paraphernalia, all creating a vision of splendour meant to rival that of Imperial Rome.

Other notable railroad stations in the Beaux-Arts style were Chicago's Union Station, which opened in 1925, and another Union Station in

Washington, DC, which opened in 1908. Both buildings were designed by Daniel Burnham and confirmed the status of Beaux-Arts as the prevailing style of architecture in the United States and the preferred choice of commercial and industrial magnates. In particular, the Union Station in the federal capital comprises a huge barrel-vaulted hall inspired by the magnificent Roman Baths of Diocletian. It is complete with lunette windows at each end, statues of Roman legionnaires on duty over the main concourse entrance, and allegorical sculptural groups depicting some of the ingredients necessary for a successful American industrial economy: agriculture, electricity, fire, freedom, imagination and engineering.

❊ Greek revival: a style for the Establishment

By about 1863, the French Second Empire design, an early form of the Beaux-Arts style which had arrived in England as a result of the Anglo-French alliance made during the Crimean War 1853–56, was regarded, predictably, as being irrelevant and too ostentatious. In particular, the mansard steeply sloped flat-topped roofs, often with crowned metal fencing and over-ornate window reveals (see figs 16 and 17) was considered by the English to be too exuberant. Instead, when and where classical ideals were required they preferred an English Renaissance mannerism, originating in the 17th century with Sir Christopher Wren. Such buildings were dressed in Portland stone, a finish adopted by the Establishment as befitting what it perceived to be its universally accepted air of dignity.

A classical style, known as the Greek Revival, was made popular by architects such as Alexander Thompson (1817–75), who built Greek-styled structures in Glasgow and Edinburgh – the so-called Athens of the North. St Pancras Church (1819–22) in London, designed by William Inwood (1771–1843), was

freely based on the Erechtheion Temple (see pp.8–10) and remains a fine example of how this style was applied to ecclesiastical buildings. The Ionic Screen at Hyde Park Corner in London (c.1825), designed by Decimus Burton (1800–81) is another faithful exploration of Greek architectural ideals.

The Greek Revival, as opposed to the late Renaissance style, adopted a more authentic and serious adaptation of Greek architectural form represented at, for example, the British Museum, London (1823–47; by Robert Smirke), and Valhalla temple near Regensburg (1831–42; by Leopold von Klenze). By contrast, Neoclassical structures often included design details that were never used by the ancient Greeks. For example, the Neoclassical Fitzwilliam Museum, Cambridge (built 1837–47; started by George Basevi and completed after his death by Professor Cockerell) has Corinthian capitals on top of corner pilasters (square pillars or columns attached to a wall). Although an Egyptian innovation and used at the temple of Saqqara, pilasters were not really used extensively by the Greeks, and corner pilasters never existed in the manner applied at the Fitzwilliam Museum.

The Greek Revival reached its apotheosis around 1840 but was not adopted by the Establishment to reflect the Victorian image, being mainly restricted for use in collegiate or cultural institutions. Its final interpretation was in the designs for St George's Hall in Liverpool in 1840–54, by H. L. Elmes (1814–47). The structure was completed by Sir Robert Rawlinson with internal decoration and completion by Emeritus Professor Charles Cockerell (1788–1863) who did much throughout his academic life to promote the acceptance of classical ideals he observed on his Grand Tour of ancient Greece in 1812.

The Neoclassical designs of the early Victorian period, however, were eventually displaced by the Neo-Gothic style (see Chapter 2), which was used on most important buildings such as the St Pancras Hotel and the new Palace

Fig. 17

Railway Station, Slough, Berkshire,
1854, Isambard Kingdom Brunel

This railway station was designed and
built by the great railroad engineer
Isambard Kingdom Brunel in the style of
early Beaux- Arts. Beaux-Arts enjoyed
a passing acceptance in England during
the Anglo–French alliance in the Crimea
war. In this building Brunel adapted the
Beaux-Arts style to suit English tastes,
replacing the typical severe French linear
mansard roof and opulent decoration with
gently a curved roof crowned with metal
fencing, and extensive glazed surfaces.

of Westminster, both in London. However, Classical-inspired designs were revived again towards the end of the Victorian era. It seemed an appropriate idiom to reflect Britain's imperial reach, which by then far exceeded that of Ancient Rome.

❀ French style in Britain: a short experiment

An exception to the prevailing architectural styles could be found in the designs proposed by the British military engineer Captain Francis Fowke for the Exhibition Building of 1862. The completed structure clearly reflected the Second Empire architectural style from France. During the reign of Napoleon III (1851–70) the French Second Empire style was the equivalent of the High Victorian Gothic Revival in England in the same period. It preceded and in some respects could be seen as the inspiration for the Beaux-Arts movement. Second Empire was accepted to an extent in England because of the Anglo-French alliance in the Crimean war of the mid-1850s. This led to a tolerance among the English of what was usually regarded as the highly decorative and ostentatious French approach to design, which was normally unacceptable to English tastes. Captain Fowke incorporated Second Empire traits – very early Beaux-Arts references in the form of curved, steep mansard roofs – to each of the end pavilions of his Exhibition Building, punctuated with decorated lucarnes (small, round dormer windows) on each upper roof attic elevation. A good example of the mansard roof is the one incorporated into the design of Slough railway station in England.

The designs for the Exhibition Building were realised and the building rapidly constructed in 1862. However, the Prime Minister, Lord Palmerston, intervened. The land upon which the Exhibition Building of 1862 stood was acquired for the nation in order to utilise the existing building as a museum. An appropriate enabling Act of Parliament received royal assent and became law. However, a consecutive Act needed to purchase the actual building from its owners and convert it into a *de facto* new Natural History Museum, failed to reach the statute book. In retaliation its owners demolished the building! Following Francis Fowke's death in 1865, the architect Alfred Waterhouse (1830–1905) was engaged to construct a new building on the site. He modified Fowke's plans and built the present Romanesque–Gothic-style Natural History Museum in South Kensington in London. However, it is possible that had the Exhibition Building of 1862 survived then this early form of Second Empire architecture might have flourished in England.

The railway engineer Isambard Kingdom Brunel (1806–59) incorporated elements of the Second Empire style, still evident today on the roof, in his designs for Slough railway station (1858) in England. His design for the station was based upon the Pavilion de Richelieu built in 1654 that forms part of the Louvre.

Ultimately, the Victorians could not quite bring themselves to fully adopt the Beaux-Arts style. They rejected the standard steep short mansard roof with its straight lines, preferring instead the curved roof covered with fish-scale patterned tiles evident at Slough station. Some buildings did, however, incorporate certain features from the Second Empire style, including cresting – ornate metal railings crowning the roof – and lucarnes; both are features used at the Exhibition Building of 1862 and at Slough railway station.

❀ Gothic revival: a High Victorian favourite

When it came to building, Gothic was the preferred style of commerce and of the Establishment in Britain. However, in 1865 the British Government, headed by Lord Palmerston, rejected Gothic designs of 1860 for the new Foreign Office by architect Sir George Gilbert Scott as unsuitable, insisting instead on Italian

Fig. 18. *St Pancras Hotel, London, Sir Gilbert Scott, 1868–76*

St Pancras Hotel, formerly the Midland Grand Hotel, closed in 1935, becoming railway offices, when the building was known as the St Pancras Chambers. The offices were vacated in 1985, and the building has been refurbished back into a hotel and duplex apartments.

Fig. 19. *John O'Connor,*
From Pentonville Road Looking West:
Evening, *1884, oil on canvas*
Photo: © Museum of London

The magnificence of the St Pancras Hotel
building was captured by John O'Connor
in his painting, From Pentonville Road
Looking West: Evening, which shows its
pinnacles, turrets and spires reaching up
into the autumnal skies at sunset.

Renaissance. Despite this apparent setback Gothic had already established itself, from 1836 onwards, as the dominant style of the Victorian era after Sir Charles Barry's successful application of Gothic style, ably assisted by the indefatigable Augustus Pugin (1812–52), at the new Palace of Westminster in London.

The Gothic style was given further impetus as the appropriate idiom for the design of buildings for the emerging middle classes, which grew with the new industrial and commercial wealth. This is evident in the construction of hospitals, prisons, offices, theatres and country houses, where Gothic designs were applied in order to invest a building with an aura of history, and especially at public schools, most of which were founded only as recently as the early 19th century.

The original architectural concept for the St Pancras Hotel by Sir George Gilbert Scott first appeared in the design for a country house in Nottinghamshire called Kelham Hall (completed in 1861). Scott modified the concept by expanding the scope of those designs when submitting his proposal for the new Foreign Office in Whitehall. Eventually, these designs were rejected by Lord Palmerston, who wanted the Foreign Office to be built in an Italianate classical style. Subsequently, in 1867, the London Midland Railway commissioned Scott to build their new hotel and railway terminus in the parish of St Pancras in London, for which Scott successfully applied those rejected Gothic designs based on Kelham Hall.

The Scott family included Sir George Gilbert Scott (1811–78) who designed the St. Pancras Hotel (figs 12 and 18). His eldest son, George Gilbert Scott junior (1839–97) underwent a mental collapse and died insane whilst living in one of the towers of the St. Pancras Hotel. George Gilbert Scott Junior's son, Sir Giles Gilbert Scott (1880–1960) was the architect of the Liverpool Anglican Cathedral (1901). He also deigned Battersea Power Station in London (1937; fig. 23, p.59) Bankside Power

Station, now the Tate Modern Gallery also in London (1963) and the classic English K2 red telephone box (designed 1935). In turn, his brother, Adrian Gilbert Scott (1882–1963), was commissioned to reduce the ambitious size of Sir Edwin Lutyens' Catholic Metropolitan Cathedral at Liverpool – the Ghost Cathedral.

The completion of the St Pancras Hotel in London confirmed the Gothic Revival style as the accepted manner of the most important buildings of the High Victorian period. Though built as a premier hotel at the height of the Victorian era, with the first hydraulic elevators and other facilities which were innovative for the time, by 1935 the St Pancras Hotel had become obsolete, superseded by more modern, better-appointed equivalents. Thereafter the building lapsed into subordinate use, instead becoming offices for the London Midland and Scottish Railway, or LMS, as it was known, and later the British Railways Board. In 1980 it finally closed its doors to the world. Sealed from intrusion, its empty corridors and vast grand halls giving evidence of a lost era of opulence, it assumed an almost legendary *Titanic* status. The grandeur of the building was captured in John O'Connor's famous painting, *St Pancras Hotel and Station from Pentonville Road* (1884), showing its pinnacles, turrets and spires reaching up to the autumnal skies at sunset (opposite).

❦ The Ghost Cathedral: religious rivalry

It was not only commercial corporations who sought to construct buildings of staggering ambition. The church in the Victorian era may have seen a diminution in its authority, but it was still the focus of respect for those who continued to believe in Scripture. To reinforce this attitude, the Catholic and Anglican Churches in early 20th-century England each embarked on ambitious plans to build churches on a scale to deliberately make statements about the importance of faith.

In 1850 legislation was passed in the UK to allow Roman Catholics to practice their faith in public. To celebrate this achievement it was widely perceived that a Cathedral should be constructed – a fact noted by the Anglican Church, who were at the same time considering designs for a cathedral of their own. Not wishing to be out-done in size or magnificence by the Roman Catholics, the Anglicans appointed Sir Giles Gilbert Scott (see p.49) as their architect. The foundation stone for the new Anglican cathedral was laid in 1904 by the English king, Edward VII, and the main structure consecrated in 1924.

In 1930 Sir Edwin Lutyens was awarded the commission to design and construct a Romanesque-style Roman Catholic cathedral in Liverpool. His brief for the Metropolitan Cathedral of Christ the King was quite simply to build 'the largest Cathedral in the world', without doubt to rival the Anglican Cathedral, by now partially built. The proposed height was to be 160 m (520 ft) dominated by a 50 m (170 ft) diameter dome – bigger than St Peter's Basilica at Rome. The height of the Anglican Cathedral was 100 m (330 ft).

Lutyens was experienced in designing large, impressive structures, including the Cenotaph in Whitehall, London (1920) and the expansive Viceroy's Palace in Delhi (1920–31), which was built on a monumental scale to impress the world as the new capital of British imperial India. He is best known for his powerful monument to the fallen of the Great War at the Thiepval Memorial, in France. This 30 m (95 ft) high memorial is a series of interlocked supporting arches, some at right angles to each other, creating a spacious but significant structure. The ideas demonstrated in the memorial were also incorporated into the Catholic cathedral's main entrance porch on the east elevation. Had they been realised, the doors to this porch would have been the largest doors ever created.

Although in 1933 work was begun on the foundations, construction was never fully realised due to changes in Diocesan priorities and general economic depression during the 1930s, which led to an escalation in building costs making the scheme unfeasible. Only the massive plinth, which incorporates the crypts and Pontifical Hall, was formed. Today the plinth is exposed and can be seen rising from the ground; an indication of the scope of the proposed cathedral superstructure (see opposite), its outline creating the ghost of the Cathedral that was never built.

After the Second World War, revised costs to complete the Cathedral were found to be inordinate. Adrian Gilbert Scott, brother of the architect of the Anglican Cathedral and grandson of the architect of the St. Pancras Hotel (see p.49) was commissioned to reduce the size of Lutyens' plan. He called for the retention only of the massive dome – yet to be built – and two completed pyramids on the existing plinth. This reduction was subsequently rejected and Sir Frederick Gibberd's smaller concrete structure ultimately built upon Sir Edwin Lutyens' plinth, and eventually consecrated in 1962.

Both cathedrals were intent on making huge statements to their faith by building on a monumental scale not seen since Classical antiquity and the Middle Ages.

Fig. 20.

Ghost Cathedral, Liverpool
unbuilt, Sir Edward Lutyens

Had it been built, Lutyens' Metropolitan
Cathedral of Christ the King would
have been the largest cathedral in the
world. This drawing shows how it would
have appeared.

CHAPTER 4

From Mayan temples to buildings lying on their backs: ferroconcrete structures

❀ Early use of ferroconcrete: a turning point in technology and design

Industrial buildings throughout the United States are almost as impressive in their monumental power as the structures of Ancient Egypt. After the Civil War, commerce and industry settled down to recover business and promote progress. This involved a massive building programme throughout the Union, funded by business and the federal government. Concrete was seen as a very adaptable and cheap building material and consequently its use became widespread, especially in America.

The development of ferroconcrete for building purposes came about in the United States around 1890 with the construction of the refinery of the Pacific Coast Borax Company, the Stanford Museum and the California Academy of Sciences, all designed by E.L. Ransome. This marked an important turning point in the development of building technology and design. Not since the construction of the gigantic cathedrals of the Middle Ages had there been such a profound acceptance of a new technology, with its implication for construction – in that case the arch and flying buttress, which allowed those massive buildings to achieve new heights and lightness of structure. Ferroconcrete was fabricated by pouring liquid concrete into timber-shuttering moulds around internal iron or steel reinforcement bars, creating a material capable of withstanding large compressive and tensile forces. Many tons of concrete could be poured into a single mould in one go and an entire structure could be cast as a single monolithic unit. This conferred a formidable integral strength to the structure, making it very difficult to damage or destroy (see Beckton Gasworks, pp.58 and 66).

Whilst the development of ferroconcrete technology was rooted in the 19th century, its application was significantly advanced during the First World War when it was used to make defensive concrete bunkers to protect soldiers from increasingly lethal bombardment and explosion. This idea was taken up by the French and reached its apogee in the Maginot Line, a series of elaborate fortified ferroconcrete bunkers constructed to deal with the later threat posed by an imminent Second World War.

German, too, built ferroconcrete bunkers. Indeed they became an integral part of German military architecture, especially in the period leading up to the 1939–45 war. The experience gained in the construction of bunkers during the Great War had demonstrated the potential of hardened ferroconcrete. During the interwar period ferroconcrete technology was applied throughout Germany on a variety of peacetime projects, such as the AEG Turbine Factory in Berlin and the Einstein Tower in Potsdam near Berlin.

Elsewhere in Europe and the world, the use of ferroconcrete for non-industrial and military structures was taken up more slowly than in Germany. Structural engineers mainly designed buildings using the ferroconcrete technique as

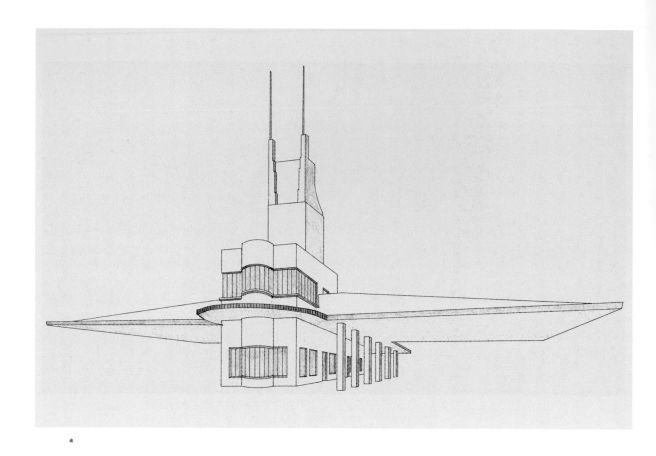

Fig. 21.

Gasoline Station, B-52, USA

The design of this building suggests
aviation more than highway architecture.
The building shows what slender forms
can be achieved by using ferroconcrete,
including the construction of cantilevered
floating masonry forms that would be
impossible to achieve using other materials
without applying awkward supporting
beams. The application of ferroconcrete
allows for the marshalling of the powerful
compressive and tensile forces inherent
in ferroconcrete structures.

an opportunity to achieve structural innovation. In addition to conferring massive tensile strength upon structures, making them extremely stable and inert, ferroconcrete allowed the formation of minimalist structures such as the bridge built by Robert Maillart in 1936 over the River Arve near Geneva. There the bridge piers have been trimmed down to minimal proportions, which was only possible because of the innate strength of ferroconcrete.

Ferroconcrete opened the way for the imaginative and innovative design of new structures (see the gasoline station opposite) because it eliminated the need for previously visible elements such as iron girders and beams. It also allowed designers to enclose vast spaces. For example, concrete piers were able to support a thin 65sq. m (700sq. ft) area of concrete roofing at Otto Wagner's Post Office Savings Bank in Vienna, built between 1904 and 1906. Later Peter Behrens (1868–1940), who understood the real significance of the expressive forces concealed in materials such as steel and glass, demonstrated his skill in his AEG Turbine Building in Berlin (designed in 1909), which has a concrete roof area measuring 167sq. m (1800sq. ft).

Such achievements were unprecedented, but ferroconcrete could be readily applied to achieving such results, and was easily adaptable for use with large areas of steel-framed glazed walls. This solution was later applied by architect Walter Gropius (1883–1969; see p.75) and the Bauhaus Movement when constructing the Bauhaus buildings at Dessau in 1925, and, in 1911, to the construction of the Royal Liver Building in Liverpool by Walter Aubrey Thomas (1859–1934), which until superseded by the Hoover Dam in 1935 was the largest reinforced poured concrete structure ever built.

New designs: fluid concrete forms

The monolithic ferroconcrete structures of the early 20th century emphasised the opening up of space, as opposed to the walling in of volume typical of buildings from the 19th century. The ability to form concrete quickly and cheaply into three-dimensional shapes made it the preferred choice of material for designers anxious to create distinctive new forms. Erich Mendelsohn's (1887–1953) Einstein Tower at Potsdam (built in 1920–21) near Berlin, Hoffmann's Stoclet Palace of 1911 (see fig. 36, p.79), Walter Gropius and Adolf Meyer's Fagus Building (1911–13), and later the Bauhaus buildings at Dessau in 1925, are the result of this rapid progress in ferroconcrete technology and design. Inspiration came from many directions.

Mayan Revival style

In the early part of the 20th century discoveries were made about the Ancient Mayan civilisation of pre-Columbian Central America. The Mexican Revolution of 1910 also focused attention on the region and its archaeological curiosities, including Mayan ruins.

Elaborate Mayan mortuary temples in the form of step pyramids were already known to the outside world through the efforts of Stephens and Catherwood in the mid-19th century. Their discoveries included the lost city of Copán, the Temple of Tikal (built 500AD), the temple citadel at Teotihuacan (c.600AD) and especially the ancient city of Chichen Itza (c.1200AD) in the Yucatán.

Most of the temples were constructed between 500 and 1200AD, and served a variety of purposes. Their shape was based on the mountains, which were deemed the abode of the gods. Each pyramid had a ceremonial flight of steps leading to a mortuary temple located at the top of the structure. Within this sacred space a variety of rituals of deep religious significance were carried out, including human sacrifice and burial. These elaborate pyramids were erected to achieve height from the ground in order to be nearer to the celestial gods when carrying out ritual worship.

These pyramid structures were adorned with stone carvings – radiating sun rays, geometric shapes, circular patterns and animal heads – a form of decoration that exerted a strong influence on early 20th century architecture.

This pre-Columbian three dimensional art form was being applied by architects before the term Art Deco was in general use, especially by Robert Stacy-Judd (1884–1975) in California and, as early as 1904, by Frank Lloyd Wright (1867–1959) on the Larkin Building in Buffalo, New York, which exhibits three-dimensional geometric shapes. These geometric shapes were also used in 1914 on the Midway Gardens project in Chicago and the Imperial Hotel in Tokyo (1915–22). In these schemes Wright's thinking clearly anticipates the more formal consolidation of concrete geometric form that crystallised into three-dimensional-aspect Art Deco constructional designs.

Ancient Egyptian designs are another interesting source of influence on Art Deco. Here the decoration and form of the capitals on top of columns were inspired by the shape of the lotus plant bud, as can be seen in the highly polychromatic Art Deco-style Carreras Building (built in 1926; now known as Greater London House) in London, designed by M.E. & O.H. Collins. Other colourful Art Deco buildings include the Firestone Building (1929) and the Hoover Building (1932), both in London, by the same architectural partnership of Wallis & Gilbert. The buildings exhibit exotic detailing in their ferroconcrete formwork but remain of an indeterminate, hybrid style. The Firestone Building, demolished in 1980, hinted at Mayan influences in the upper sections of its two pavilions, while the masonry surrounding the modern clock located above the main entrance featured a Mayan sunburst and three-dimensional geometric shapes.

The number of international influences that contributed to the development of the Art Deco style owed much to the plasticity of ferroconcrete, which made complex three-dimensional shapes easily reproducible. Examples of the adaptability of this material can be seen at the Larkin Building in Buffalo, at Union Depot railroad station in Joplin, Missouri (see figs 27 and 28), in the stepped pyramid structures (now demolished) at the Golden Gate Exhibition in San Francisco (1939–40; see fig. 23, p.59) John Austin's Los Angeles City Hall (1926–8, with a Mayan stepped stone pyramid on top of its masonry tower) and Nascreno House at 27 Soho Square in London (see fig. 24, p.60).

These two elements – three-dimensional shapes and the carved decoration found on Mayan temples – combined to become the more formal Art Deco style of detailing in construction. The style provided opportunities for innovative designs easily expressed in stone or poured concrete, especially at the Hollyhock House in California (1917–21) and Unity Temple at Oak Park in Illinois (1904–06), both designed by Frank Lloyd Wright

Another aspect of Mayan temple design influence on Art Deco structures was in the actual form or massing of buildings, often in the form of truncated pyramids. Usually a building would express a series of cubes representing the actual temple on top of the pyramid. Good examples are the US Bullion Depository (see pp.83–4), at Fort Knox, Kentucky, the Museum of Contemporary Art in Sydney, the four buttress piers of the nearby Sydney Harbour Bridge, and the University of London Senate House building in England, (1932–7; Charles Holden). A way of emphasizing the cubic bulk and form was to use different building materials, typically at the Wilshire Building in Los Angeles in 1929 designed by J. and D. Parkinson. Here the structure reflects the heavy cubic aspect of the Mayan Temple – low, heavy layers in brick with striated grooved stone bands with chamfered edges delineated between other materials to produce a layered cubism.

Fig. 22.

Chichen Itza, Yucatán,
Ancient Maya civilization

A typical stepped pyramid used by ancient
Mayan priests to record, amongst other
rituals, the advent of their 584-day
calendar based on the annual cycle of the
planet Venus, considered an important
god. Religious rituals, including human
sacrifice, were also carried out – usually
in the temple located at the top of the
series of steps which form the pyramid
structure. The shape of the temple, low,
solid and cubic, provided inspiration for
the monumental block-style Art Deco
buildings of the 1930s, typified in figs 7,
35 and 36.

Art Deco was adopted almost universally, especially in the United States during the 1930s, when many massive concrete structures were built, such as the Genesee Valley Trust Building (see p.97) and the Chrysler Building, both in New York (see pp.88–9). As the use of ferroconcrete became increasingly widespread, so the application of Art Deco design in concrete became more common in architecture.

An example of three-dimensional geometrical shaping can be found in the structure of Union Depot railroad station at Joplin, Missouri. The designs for this station, dating from 1911, are an early application of Art Deco motifs based on religious symbols from the ancient Mayan civilisation. This could be seen in the intricate detailing to the concrete formwork of one of the station's pavilions.

In contrast to this is the huge ferroconcrete temple at Rexburg in Idaho. Built as a church, its plain undecorated massiveness reflects the ferroconcrete industrial grain silos that are a prominent feature in Idaho and the American Midwest.

Ferroconcrete was almost universal in its application across a wide spectrum of design in commercial, industrial and residential building. The use of this material meant that an entire building could be cast as a single monolithic unit. This was certainly the case at Union Depot railroad station in Joplin, but more spectacularly at the Beckton complex of ferroconcrete structures in London.

❀ Indestructible structures: the application of ferroconcrete at Beckton Gasworks

Beckton Gasworks was founded in 1868 as a production facility for the manufacture of town gas to serve what was then the largest metropolis in the world. The works were located in the East End of London and occupied an area of about 550 acres. The site included chemical works and recovery installations, creating the largest gas production facility in the world.

The site at Beckton comprises several building types necessary for a variety of manufacturing processes. These include such exotic structures as the Horizontal Retort Plant, the Triple Pavilion Building, the Carburetted Water Gas Plant, the Gas Dehydration Plant, the Boiler House, the Power Station and the Intermediary Building.

The majority of the buildings are typical in design of 1930s industrial architecture, tending to be massive and monolithic both in scale and structure. The use of ferroconcrete in their construction is particularly apposite given the essential functions of these buildings. Ferroconcrete produces remarkably strong, monolithic structures that are very difficult to damage or destroy – which can in fact sustain major damage whilst remaining intact.

This capacity was demonstrated dramatically on the night of 7 September 1940 during a massive air raid by the Luftwaffe, and in subsequent raids, when at least two hundred bombs exploded on the site. Production of gas was intermittently interrupted. However, the buildings remained structurally intact despite their interior fittings and machinery being destroyed by fire or by bomb damage.

Ferroconcrete structures behave in a different manner to brick buildings when subjected to an explosion. In a building constructed of bricks cemented together the structural integrity of the building is based upon the structural compressive forces acting vertically downward upon each individual brick. The weight of the building is therefore transmitted down through the brickwork into the foundations, creating stability. The sudden release of energy from an explosion results in a supersonic shockwave travelling horizontally. This causes the compressive forces acting downward through the brickwork to fail, profoundly compromising

Fig. 23.

A single tower of Battersea Power Station, London, 1930s, Giles Gilbert Scott, and an allegorical pyramid from the Golden Gate Exhibition, San Francisco, 1939

Built as the main entrance to the 1939–40 Golden Gate Exhibition in San Francisco, this Art Deco pyramid, was one of a pair of three-dimensional Art Deco fantasies inspired by Mayan structures. Adjacent is an isolated chimney from the London power station with stepped detailing at the upper level.

Fig. 24.

No. 27 Soho Square, London

This Art Deco building has a monumental
entrance canopy in concrete formwork.
The geometrical design of the canopy
shows clearly the versatility of concrete
in forming complex shapes.

Fig. 25.

Railroad Station, Joplin, Missouri, 1911, Louis Curtiss

This ferroconcrete Union Pacific Railroad structure, complete with exuberant neurotic detailing, was built in 1911. The building displays early Art Deco designs in the concrete formwork, which reflect decoration found in funereal temples of the ancient Mayans. Joplin Railroad Station was regarded as an important depot of the Union Pacific Railroad because it linked the three main railroads serving the southwestern United States: the Kansas City Southern, the Missouri-Kansas-Texas and the Santa Fe. The significance of the building is expressed in its elaborate ornamentation and Art Deco symbolism. The basic mannerism of the building is influenced by Frank Lloyd Wright's Prarie school of design, which emphasised low, horizontal buildings that hug the ground, rather than the verticality of Victorian or Neoclassical structures that were in vogue at the time.

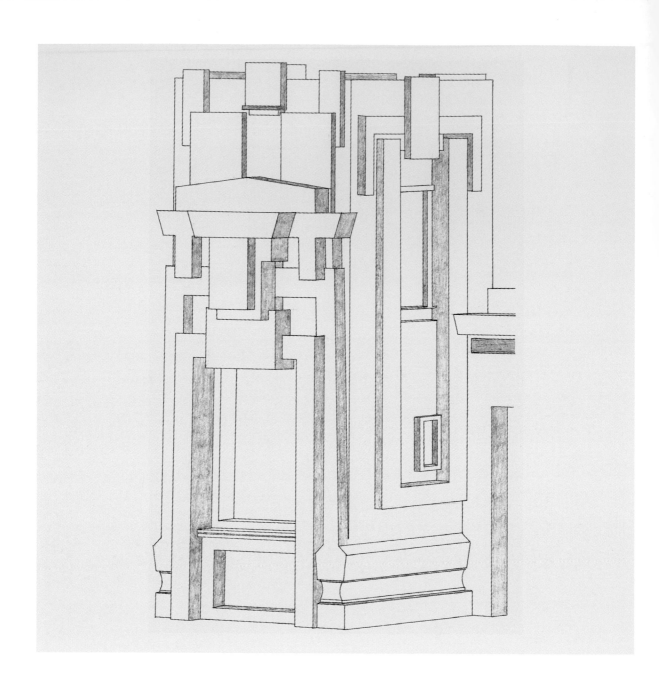

Fig. 26.
Railroad Station, Joplin, Missouri
(detail of a pavilion),
1911, Louis Curtiss

This detail shows the complex formwork
that can be achieved in poured concrete.
This early Art Deco design was inspired by
the decoration found on the ancient Mayan
pyramids of Central America.

Fig. 27.

Temple at Rexburg, Idaho, 2007, LDS

This ferroconcrete structure is in fact
a place of worship, although it resembles
more a typical grain silo structure of
the Mid-western United States. It shows
clearly the adaptability of poured concrete
in creating large, interesting structurally
integral forms.

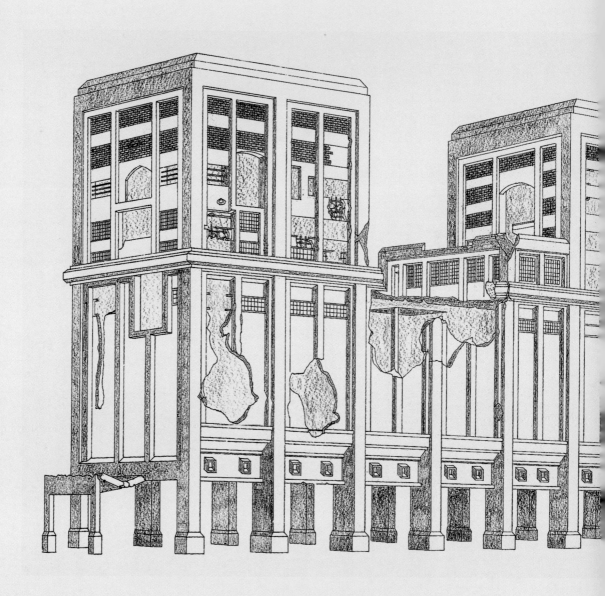

Fig. 28
Triple Pavilion Building, Beckton,
London, 1926, GL&C Co.

These buildings formed part of the
extensive gas production facility located in
east London adjacent to the Royal Docks
complex. They were an example of early
industrial design, using ferroconcrete
as the main material to confer massive
strength to the structure. Heavily bombed
during World War II, though not quite
to oblivion, they remained structurally
intact until their demolition in 1998. The
appearance of these buildings during those
intervening years gave them a minatory
and gaunt look making them a preferred
location for film directors.

the structure of the building and causing the masonry to collapse into rubble.

In the case of reinforced concrete, the reverse is applicable because this material behaves as an integral whole. The steel rods and mesh can redirect structural forces instantly around damaged or indeed missing masonry. Despite concerted bombing during numerous air raids which resulted in whole sections of the structure being literally blown away, those parts of buildings at the Beckton Gasworks that did not suffer direct hits remained intact and upright. In particular the Triple Pavilion Building and an adjacent building were subject to bombing and intense fire, yet still remained intact and upright.

Where, however, deliberate undermining of the structure has taken place, reinforced concrete behaves in a characteristically bizarre manner. Where the foundation piers, upon which the structure is built, have been removed or extensively damaged, then the weight ratio of the building shifts and the structure compensates by quite literally rolling over, often intact, onto its back!

At Beckton one building, now demolished, the Ancillary Plant, had rolled 112° away from its vertical mean, the correct upright position of a building. Previously supported on its foundation columns, these columns now pointed upward to the sky. This fact serves to emphasize the point that reinforced concrete buildings are inherently difficult to reduce to rubble.

Moreover, because of their enduring capacity to absorb damage, however inflicted, the buildings were useful in creating a backdrop for various films. The buildings in their current minatory state are still redolent of a war zone. Punctuating a desolate landscape as they once did, those burned-out wrecks looked forever dead, including those on their backs, making them a preferred film location. In 1995 continued planning permission was granted to develop the site into a commercial development.

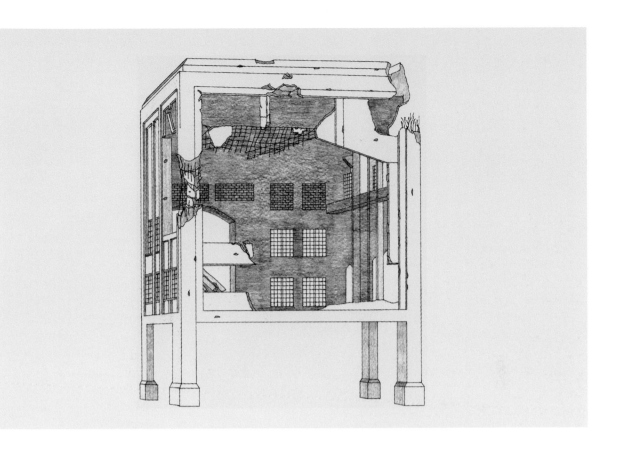

Fig. 29.
Intermediary Building, Beckton,
London, 1926, GL&C Co.

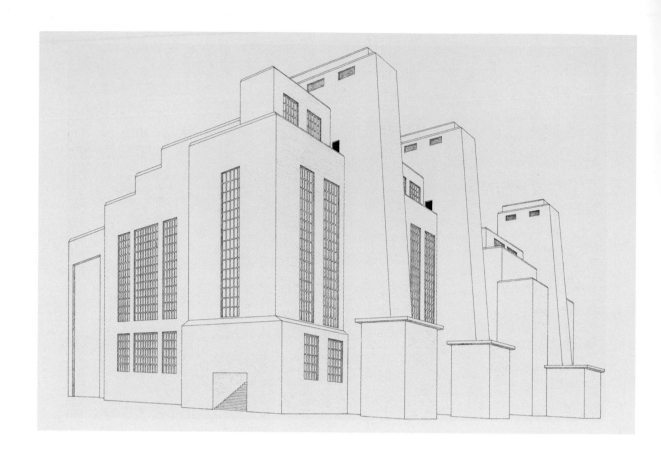

Fig. 30.
Carburetted Water Gas Plant
Beckton, London, 1926, GL&C Co.

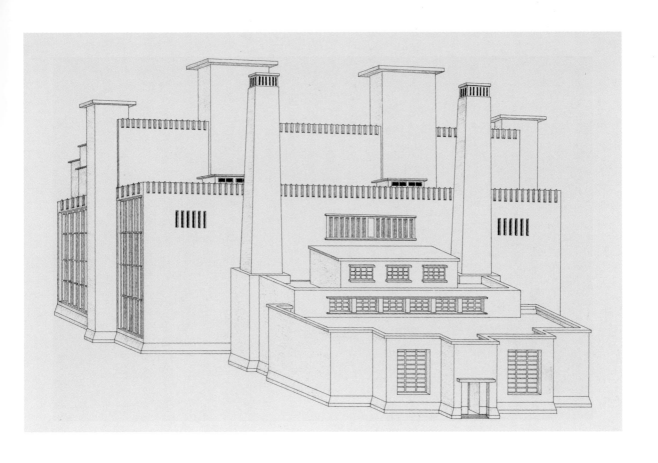

Fig. 31.
*Boiler House, Beckton, London,
1926, GL&C Co.*

CHAPTER 5

Psychology of Buildings: from modern temple design to Freud

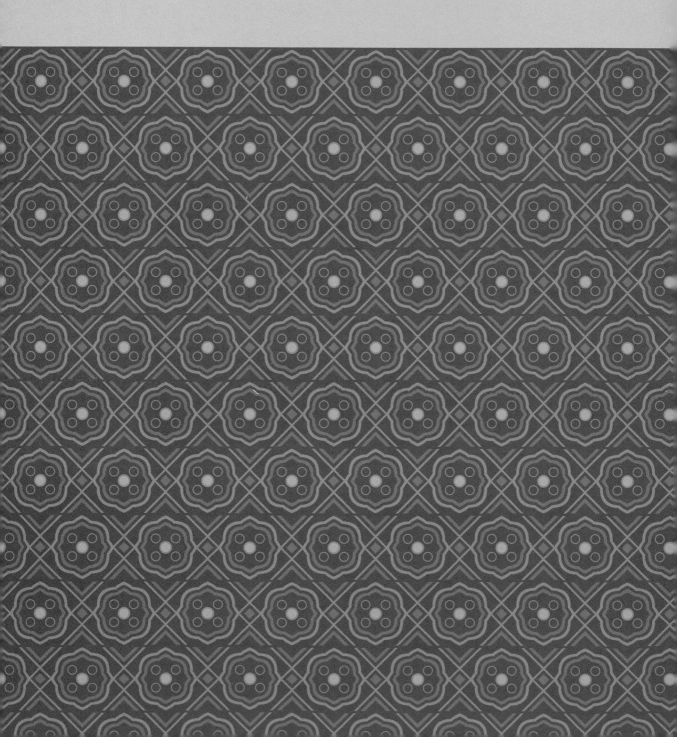

✾ Psychology of buildings: a new awareness

Some buildings are designed in a very specific way to instil anxiety or apprehension about what they hold within their precincts and away from our gaze. A fortress is one readily understood example of this phenomenon, as is a castle. There are buildings, such as the infamous Bastille, which have deliberately propagated a reputation for fear or a dread at being admitted to their interior.

Other buildings, while not designed to instill dread, can be equally intimidating, although this may not have been the intention of the architect.

A case in point is fig. 34 (p.76), a temple ostensibly built as a place for worship. Its fortress-like symbolism may be subtle, but is no less disturbing for that. The whole edifice is massive and built on a high plinth making it seem unapproachable: it does not welcome, but rather deters visitors. Usually, where a building is designed to impose itself onto the district it is constructed to monumenal proportions, on the basis that it is all pervading. A bungalow, in this respect, would fail to impress or instill dread in quite the same way.

The same case can be made of fig. 35 (p.77), a postmodern office building in Slough. Again, certain building elements create a mannerism that is not necessarily a deliberately designed detail, especially when considering the role of the steps leading up to the building flanked by two towers.

The fact that buildings can affect people psychologically is better understood today than it was in Georgian or Victorian times, when the dynamics of space and construction, and their effects upon the mind, were hardly considered. This lack of understanding was demonstrated most grotesquely at Bethlehem Royal Hospital, better known as Bedlam, a Georgian institution based at Moorgate in London. Built by Robert Hooke (1635–1703), polymath and inventor of the spirit level, its architecture was considered by the diarist John Evelyn (1620–1706) to be beautiful, and similar in design to the Tuileries Palace in Paris. Nonetheless, it was an institution to house the insane and socially unfit.

There existed no formal systematic diagnosis of an inmate's condition, nor any attempt to alleviate their mental or physical suffering through treatment. Indeed, whipping patients was common practice until discouraged in the 1790s. Instead the regime was geared to keeping inmates off the street for their own and the public's protection. In 1815 Bedlam was relocated to Lambeth and rebuilt to the designs of architect, Lewis Cubitt (1799–1883) with later additions by Sydney Smirke (1798–1877), brother of the designer of the British Museum, Sir Robert Smirke (1781–1867). One of its most esteemed inpatients, in his last few months of life, was the interior designer who had worked indefatigably upon the new Palace of Westminster, Augustus Welby Pugin (1812–52). Later, in 1863 the seriously criminally insane were transferred to Broadmoor, a Victorian establishment located outside London. Neither

72

Fig. 32.

Bastille Fortress, Paris, 14th century

This drawing is based on an imaginative reconstruction of the interior of the Bastille by the Venetian engineer and engraver, Giambattista Piranesi (1720–78). The Bastille was the infamous prison to which French revolutionaries were sent with little or no chance of being released. The Bastille became synonymous with state-organised terror – a reputation the state did little to diminish because it served its purpose in checking any public expression of dissent.

establishment at the time did much to address the problems of mental illness, and in fact merely treated patients as prisoners to be kept away from the public for a period of time.

The conditions in both establishments were similar, the large dormitories having small windows and very basic furniture. Some inmates were chained to the wall, while others were allowed to roam around the building. Bedlam at one stage was considered a tourist attraction where visitors were allowed access to view the inmates arrayed in cages. In 1770 this practice was abandoned because it disturbed the peace and quietude of the inmates by subjecting them to diversion and sport for the amusement of spectators. Thereafter admission to the privileged few would be by ticket only!

Access to fresh air was via the courtyard. Sanitary conditions were equal to the worst prevailing in the poorer reaches of society. The Victorian attitude was consistent with how they dealt with patients, namely as a charge on the public purse to whom only the basic necessities would be offered. The concept of a social health service was alien to both the Victorians and the Georgians. The building itself conformed to Victorian thinking about mental illness and life in general, especially with regard to keeping the world out by allowing only small windows (though it ought to be said that innovations in artificial illumination during this period in the form of gas, and later electric light made this less of an issue). However, in a small concession to basic human compassion, the Church was allowed to intercede to assist the inmates if it so wished.

Much thought was given in the late 19th and early 20th centuries to the impact buildings could have on people and their environment. An important figure in this area was the architect Alvar Aalto (1898–1976), for whom the way a building might affect a person's response to an enclosed environment was a primary concern, as can be seen in his sanatorium building at Paimio in Finland, built in 1929.

Fig. 33. *Vigo House, London,
1923, Burnet & Tate*

Located in Regent Street, London, Vigo
House has a basic Neoclassical style,
but the way the entablature progresses
upward from the roof-line architrave
suggests a repressed monumentalism.

The 20th century: architecture and the arts

The Deutscher Werkbund was an association of German architects, artists and designers, founded in 1907, and included Peter Behrens and Josef Hoffmann among its members. It was the forerunner of Walter Gropius's Bauhaus school, and among its aims was the intention to increase the amount space and light in their buildings through the use of glazed walls.

Hoffmann's masterpiece is the Stoclet Palace. This building indicates a return to classicism in style but used ferroconcrete in its construction in order to span large internal spaces within the building and allow light to flow unimpeded. Other artists assisted in Hoffmann's design for the palace and the artist Gustav Klimt provided some of the internal decorative finishes. The building remains an important example of integration of the arts emanating out of the Wiener Werkstätte, a community of Viennese visual artists.

From 1890 to 1914 Berlin and Vienna were lively cosmopolitan centres of intellectual debate where artists, philosophers and creative individuals mixed in society with ease allowing ideas to cross-fertilise. The composer Gustav Mahher 1860-1911 was a prominent member of Viennese society and met with other leading figures at the time. One such person whom Mahler consulted in April 1910 was the psychoanalyst Sigmund Freud to get treatment for his failing relationship with his wife Alma. This in turn was brought on by Alma's affair with the twenty-eight year old architect Walter Gropius, who she married after Mahler's death in 1911.

Within society, new intellectual ideas were discussed and improved especially those relating to the psyche. It was a time where ideas about human behaviour and condition were being propounded by Freud and acted upon by Alvar Aalto in sanatorium design and by Gropius in his designs for the Fagus Works 1911 addressing space and light.

In a letter to Theodor Reik in 1935, Freud remarked that when dealing with Mahler 'No light fell at the time on the symptomatic façade of his obsessional neurosis. It was as if you would dig a single shaft through a mysterious building'. The reason for Freud's departure from medical terminology into construction analogy is because intellectuals considered disciplines of interest other than their own imitating the Renaissance ideal. Previously Mahler had been involved with the construction of the Munich Exhibition Hall 1906 which was built using the new ideas as re-enforced concrete, iron columns and fabricated windows. In order to 'create adequate daylight and space the building supported large areas of glass and is based on simplicity and restraint' as described in Die Ausstellung of 1908. The reason was to premiere Mahler's mighty Eighth Symphony that calls for huge orchestral forces involving a thousand persons.

Because of the free movement of artists, designers and intellectuals, the arts were fusing together to address innovative concepts expressed in architecture and the Humanities including the new science of psychoanalysis and the implication of hysteria by Freud. Music, especially by Schoenberg in his twelve tone regime, Zemlinsky and Mahler fig 38, played a significant role in exploring with other artists unconventional ideas and form in endeavouring to understand the human condition. Mahler was acquainted with Gropius and Carl Moll who was in the process of designing a house for Mahler near Vienna. Space was of concern to architects such as Josef Hoffmann, Gropius and especially to Mahler since it was an important consideration in his life. He spent time trying to find an acceptable equilibrium in which to exist comfortably. Not easy with Mahler's neurotic condition as identified by Freud, even more so given his propensity for depression and pessimism, captured in his music and the adage every silver lining has a dark cloud! ✿

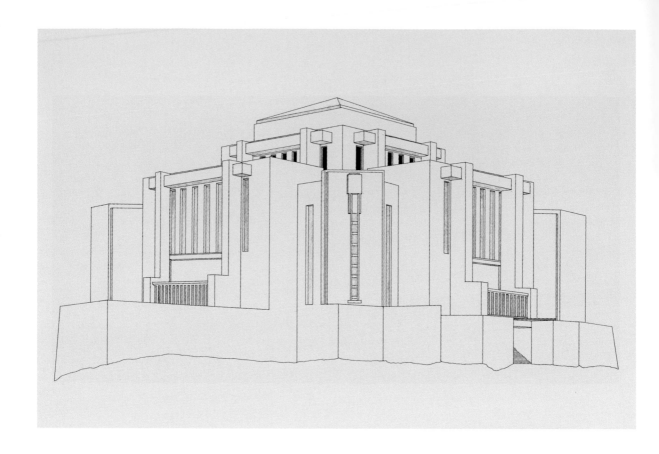

Fig. 34.
Temple, Cardston, California,
1923, LDS

Built in white granite upon an octagon plan,
this temple combines the massiveness of
Grecian architecture with Mayan influences,
seen in its pyramid-shaped silhouette.
The structure is complete with elongated
window openings and set-back terraces
that create a curiosity of activity within the
building, re-enforced by the clear fortress
style of its design. Despite being a place of
worship the mannerism of the building does
not give it a welcoming aspect.

Fig. 35.
Postmodern Building,
Slough, Berkshire

A postmodern structure built in the Art Deco style, this building has facial features and aspects of repellence expressed clearly in its façade which surmounts a series of steeply rising steps. The doors and window reveals are recessed into the structure, further confirming that tangible impression creating an increased apprehension in the visitor on approaching the building.

In building these sanatoria, Aalto and others endeavoured to understand the basic problems affecting mental health. Aalto's approach was based on a generosity with space. Light roomy spacious areas are typical, preferably with balcony access to views and air, which he hoped would create the conditions where a patient might recover or improve. Access to other people and to activity were also important considerations when planning the overall building. The use of glazed bricks was developed in order to increase the flow of light and reduce the sense of claustrophobia and hysteria to which some patients might be susceptible.

The sanatorium was built for patients recovering from tuberculosis or other illnesses. Careful consideration was given to basic concepts such as human scale, and the size and proportion of rooms, the height and width of a staircase, the height of the ceiling and access to glazed areas, providing a flow of air and light and creating a feeling of cleanliness and well-being. The building is made of white-painted ferroconcrete and built to six storeys, with cantilevered balconies giving direct access to air and landscaped views.

Other architects who explored human interaction with buildings include Otto Wagner (1841–1918), Adolf Loos (1870–1933), both Austrian, and Frank Lloyd Wright. The use of light emanating from a source not immediately visible can create in the mind of the observer a notion that there is more space than is immediately obvious or visible. Two architects in particular, Gropius (1883–1969) and Behrens (1868–1940), considered the application of light and space in their respective solutions to this challenge. Both architects explored the use of glass and steel in continuing the style of structures designed by Gustave Eiffel (1832–1923) to create huge glazed openings. Light affects the mind as much as heat affects the body; the use of glass in emphasising the opening up of space is essential. Buildings that have large glazed areas of ferro-vitreous vaulting systems, or atriums, such as

the Interdenominational Church in Milton Keynes, tend to be more attractive to people than windowless complexes where all lighting is artificial.

❈ Space and location: impact on buildings

Integral to the design of a building is its relationship to space. Consider the space inside a glass cube the size of an elevator car. Although physically unchanged, the observer's sense of the space within the cube will be qualified by the surrounding environment. For example, consider how different the space within would feel if the cube was floating in the Pacific Ocean, or sitting on a Kansas plain, or perched in a tree in the forest, or atop a skyscraper, or embedded in a mine shaft. The space within has remained constant but the external environment has changed dramatically.

It is precisely these differences that make us aware of how environment can affect space and how we perceive it. Space can also qualify a building and our response to it, even from a distance. For example, consider the Carburetted Water Gas Plant. As an industrial building it fits in well with the environment at Beckton Gasworks, which comprises several similar industrial buildings. Were that same building to be located in a field or sited in the desert, the impact of the building would change even though the building structure has not. Of course, the reverse can be true where a desert building is located within a city environment (see fig. 38, p.81).

Previous designers have endeavoured to control space by addressing the feelings of visitors in order to make their buildings successful in what they were designed to do, namely to attract people inside. Eiffel succeeded in applying the relatively new technology of ferro-vitreous vaulting systems, combining an iron frame and glass panels, to create an elongated atrium to form his Galerie des Machines for the Paris Exhibition in 1878. The

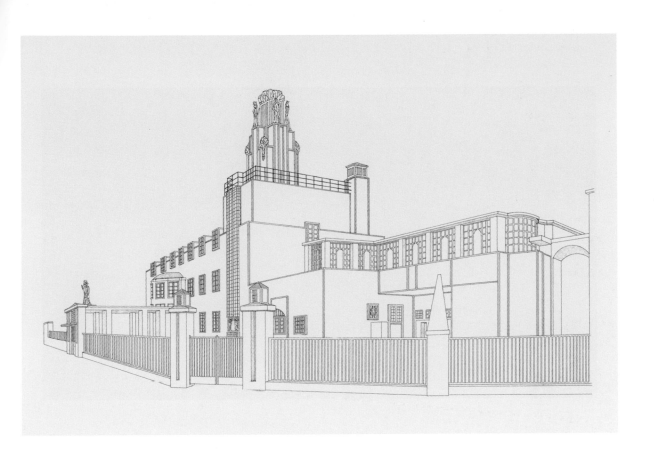

Fig. 36.
Stoclet Palace, Brussels,
1911, Josef Hoffman

This masterpiece by Josef Hoffman
made use of modern materials such as
ferroconcrete. The internal decorative
finishes were by the artist Gustav Klimt and
the Wiener Werkstätte, making this project
a good example of integration of the arts.

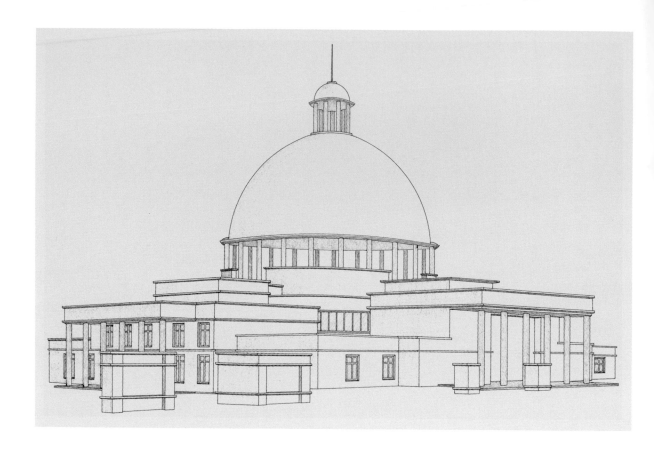

Fig. 37.

Interdenominational Church,
Milton Keynes, Buckinghamshire,
1992

This church was erected to address
a temporal vacuum, but conforms to
postmodern designs. The focus is the
elevated domed rotunda complete with
geometrical piers. The building forms
a cruciform punctuated by columns
supporting various terraces at different
levels. Should it be required, it would
be easy to successfully adapt this structure
from temporal to secular use.

Fig. 38.
Office Building
(known as Wellington Building),
St. John's Wood, London, 1986,
Newman Levinson

This building is reminiscent of the
architecture of 1920s Casablanca,
and is a modern interpretation in style
and formwork of a pavilion-type
desert building.

Fig. 39.
Galerie des Machines, Paris, 1878

The International Exhibition of 1878
was primarily intended to showcase
a series of designs to the world. Eiffel's
contribution was his design for the
Galerie des Machines, which made use of
iron and glass in the structure, echoing
the design of the Crystal Palace in 1851.

same principles that Eiffel promoted are applied by designers of shopping malls today. Unless compelled to do so, it is unlikely that shoppers would do their shopping in a subterranean concrete bunker, though they might watch a movie in such a place, because the darkness of such a space makes it appropriate for watching a film.

The concept of space can be affected by the use of a balcony, an integral part of a building that remains outside its frame. This concept appeals to most people because it allows the free movement from one environment to another through the building's fabric. Whatever its design, a building is made more interesting by the concept of the balcony or veranda. The use of such structural features in a building can increase its spatial dimensions: it offers both the experience of both being in a room inside a building, or being in a different space on the exterior of a building.

The large expanses of glass that have become a feature of so many modern buildings let in light and create the illusion of open space. A complete contrast to such buildings can be seen in structures not intended for entry by the public, for example, the structure on the roof of the Cumberland Hotel at Marble Arch in London, designed by F.J. Wills and built in 1933. There the structure was designed to reflect the structural monumentalism of a Mayan mortuary temple complex and in doing so created a vision of ethereal isolation that perhaps can be seen in fig. 40 (p.85).

To come across these buildings located in a dense rainforest in Central America would present an awesome spectacle, if not a frightening one, because of their size and location. The effects are somewhat diluted when their imitations are to be observed on top of a London hotel. However, they do serve to indicate the impact of the concept of space when out of context.

A building that is isolated has its presence amplified. This fact is exemplified at the US

Bullion Depository in Kentucky. Here space
enhances the dominant physical presence of
the building in its immediate environment.
It is no coincidence that the US bullion reserve
is housed in a fortress that is set back and
isolated for obvious security reasons. However,
the building's manner is based clearly on ancient
Mayan pyramid temple design, including motifs
surrounding the entrance door architrave (see
fig. 22, p.57), a style evolved with the intention
of instilling dread upon approaching the
structure. Similarly, a building that is located
in a city but set back in its own protected
grounds is able to impart a sense of power
and importance by being deliberately isolated.
Examples are the US Treasury building in
Washington, DC, and the Statue of Liberty on
Ellis Island in Upper New York Bay. The statue's
isolated location on this island was deliberate,
designed to impress anyone arriving in
New York by sea.

Fig. 40.

Cumberland Hotel, Marble Arch,
London, 1933, F.J. Wills

Viewed in isolation, on the top of the hotel,
this group of Art Deco structures could
almost be considered to reflect a Mayan
mortuary temple complex in its structural
monumentalism.

Fig. 41.

United States Federal Bullion
Reserve, Kentucky, 1936,
Public Buildings Administration

This building, sometimes known as
Fort Knox, is a good example of how
deliberately positioning a building in
isolation enhances the impression of
its importance and impregnability.
The mannerism of the structure containing
the bullion vault (shown here) is Art Deco,
and in its design reflects the stepped
pyramid temples of the ancient Mayan
civilization. The design of the temples was
intended to instil fear and respect amongst
the people for the Mayan gods.

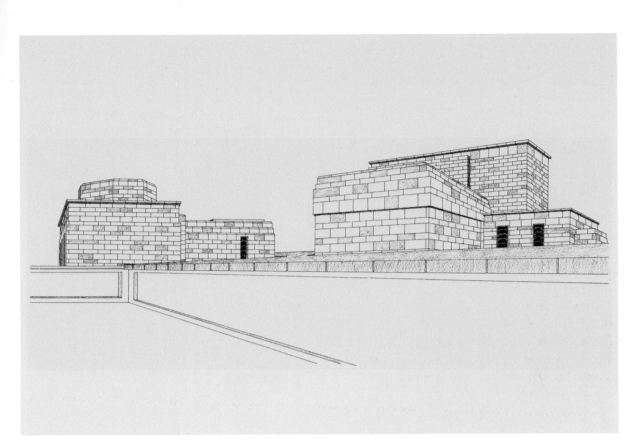

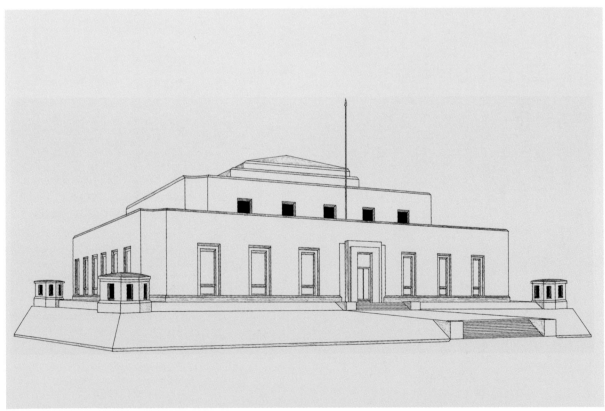

CHAPTER 6

From megalomania to an aircraft collision-proof
skyscraper: powerful buildings

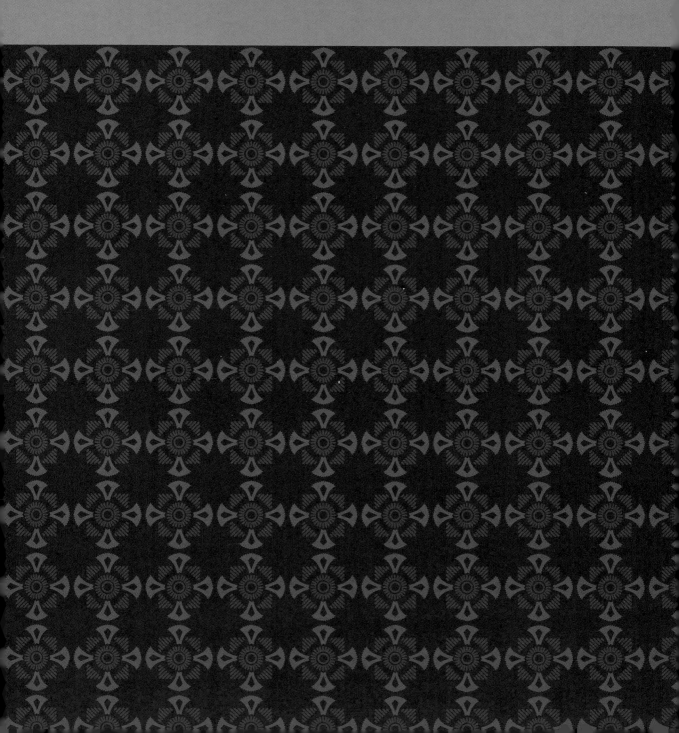

The word 'skyscraper', though a nautical term describing the uppermost sail on a three-mast rigged ship, was first applied to the tall buildings designed and constructed in Chicago by William LeBaron Jenney during the 1880s, using the cage frame technology first developed by the Victorians. These new buildings soon reached heights that had been unimaginable only a short time before. Not since the time of the great cathedrals during the Middle Ages had there been such a revolution in how buildings were constructed as that which produced the skyscraper phenomenon.

The motivating forces behind the rise of these buildings were economic and financial. A developer with a relatively small plot operating in a market where real estate is at a premium, such as New York or Chicago, will obtain a higher rental income if the building constructed on that site rises through several floors.

Two technical innovations aided this rapid development. The advent of the Otis safety elevator, first developed in the 1850s, allowed movement of persons up through the building by mechanical means using a hydraulic engine. Previously the height of a building was restricted to the maximum number of floors it could reasonably be expected that people would climb via a staircase – five, six, perhaps seven at the most. The elevator meant that all floors could be reached with ease, so that the whole building, no matter how tall, could potentially be occupied. As a result, skyscrapers were seen as economically viable

and within a few decades were proliferating throughout the United States.

The second factor was the development of an assembly-line production of steel girders, which allowed the building components of a skyscraper to be made in a foundry, typically in Pittsburgh, then transported and fabricated on site to form the building frame. This assembly-line system was later adapted and used by Henry Ford in his production of automobiles.

This innovative method of girder fabrication was first employed in the construction of the Crystal Palace in London in 1851. However, it was later finessed into what became known as the 'Chicago School' method, and not only reduced construction costs but reduced significantly the time it took to construct a skyscraper. Typically, the Empire State Building at 116m (1250ft) high took only eight months to construct, and that included the time taken to demolish the existing Waldorf-Astoria Hotel, construction of the new building and the internal fit out. The Chicago style gained universal acceptance because of these tangible and very profitable benefits.

❦ Competitive construction: into the skies

The new technology quickly allowed the height of buildings to increase dramatically, starting with the Tacoma Building in 1887–9, followed by the Monadnock Building (1889–91) and the Reliance Building (1890), all in Chicago. This principle was soon being applied to construction in Manhattan, beginning with the 11-storey Tower Building in 1888. In 1890, it was surpassed by the World Building, which rose through 18 floors, only to be topped in 1903 by the 21-storey Fuller Building on Fifth Avenue. In 1908, the 43-floor Singer Building was completed, but was overshadowed within months to the gigantic 50-storey Metropolitan Life Tower at Madison Square. This was followed by the 60-storey Woolworth Building (1911–13), referred to as the 'Cathedral of Commerce'. Indeed, direct comparison of the new skyscrapers with the great Gothic cathedrals was sometimes unavoidable, as in the case of the Chicago Tribune Tower completed in 1925, which, although representing the cutting edge of construction using building technology that epitomised the future, in its style deliberately set out to evoke Gothic excess, complete with buttresses.

This syndrome continued with the election in 1928 of President Hoover, which triggered intense speculative dealing in stock on the New York Stock Exchange. This led to the American economy over-heating, further inflating stock values. Wall Street effectively detached itself from the real economy of the United States, precipitating a stock market collapse in 1929. However, prior to that collapse, capital normally reserved for investment in industry and manufacturing was either diverted into more lucrative stock speculation, further driving up prices, or into real estate investment and the construction of tangible assets – preferably skyscrapers – to mark the land. This led to a further building frenzy culminating in the Wrigley Building in Chicago.

The race was now on as reason was abandoned and madness gripped speculators. In 1928 the automobile magnate Walter Chrysler, President of the Chrysler Corporation, commissioned the architect William van Alen to construct the tallest skyscraper in New York – if not on earth. Located on 42nd Street, it was to become the powerful Art Deco headquarters of the Chrysler

Automobile Corporation. Chrysler's wish for a landmark building that would upstage his commercial rivals, principally General Motors, was triumphantly, though briefly, fulfilled. The building was adorned with symbols of his 1929 Chrysler automobiles.

Typically, within weeks another building broke out of the ground en route to the sky, as H.C. Severence's Bank of the Manhattan Trust on Wall Street began to rise to its eventual 70 storeys. Competition between the two architects to achieve the distinction of having designed the world's tallest building was intense. Eventually, after a series of deceptions perpetrated by both architects, the erection of the 17m (185ft) long stainless-steel needle ensured that the Chrysler building rose to its final height of 77 storeys, and claim victory.

However, the Chrysler building held this title for only for a brief period before being surpassed by a structure some 59m (200ft) higher, which became the very symbol of the skyscraper. Indeed, since the tragedy of the World Trade Center, it has been once again the tallest building in New York. It was designed by William F. Lamb from the architectural firm of Shreve, Lamb & Harmon for another automobile magnate, John Jacob Raskob, President of the General Motors Corporation. His question to Lamb was, 'How high can you make it so it won't fall down?' Applying the Chicago School assembly-line method of steel fabrication, Lamb was able to deliver 1350 feet of real estate into the sky to create what for 42 years remained the tallest skyscraper in the world – the Empire State Building.

Completed in 1931, the Empire State Building rises through 102 storeys (including the tower at the top) and remains an undisputed icon for New York and a fine example of Art Deco architecture. The original designs called for an airship mooring facility, but when this proved dangerous, a metal grid communications mast was positioned on top of the tower. However, this did not prevent a US Air Force Mitchell

Fig. 42.

Chrysler Building, New York, 1930,
Walter Van Alen

This futuristic skyscraper was
commissioned by the automobile magnate
Walter Chrysler, and includes a range of
automobile symbols in its design, such as
hubcaps and eagle's heads. The tower is
crowned with an outrageous pinnacle clad
in prototype Monell stainless steel.

bomber from crashing into the 79th floor in 1945. But despite fire and serious damage, unlike the the Twin Towers, the building remained intact and was again open for business just a few days later.

The building was able to sustain such catastrophic damage and remain intact because of its steel cage-frame construction, as invented by the Victorians. This type of fabrication, a series of cubic boxes forming a cage, allows structural forces to be diverted around any damaged section of overall structural tower. The exact opposite occurred at the Twin Towers of the World Trade Center, whose construction resorted to external load-bearing external walls acting as structural elements in what is known as the tube-frame structural system. When these were exposed to high temperatures from the fires caused by the impact of the jet aircraft, the structural integrity of the exterior steel girder assembly was severely compromised, leading to a catastrophic collapse of the infrastructure.

❦ Stepped skyscrapers: distinctive Deco profiles

One aspect of Art Deco skyscraper design is an emphasis on speed. Common Art Deco motifs symbolising speed include curved, streamlined shapes and pressed-metal sheeting. Inlaid elements – usually made of wood, marble or glass – are also typical, fashioned to create a style expressing opulence and wealth. Eliel Saarinen (1873–1950) applied this approach to his unsuccessful entry for the competition to build the Chicago Tribune Tower in 1923.

One of the contributing factors affecting the massing and shape of the Empire State Building was the New York Zoning Resolution, which governed the construction of tall buildings in the city. The code was introduced in 1916 as a reaction to the impressive Woolworth Building (1911–13) and the massive Equitable Building (1915) both of which blocked out sunlight

at street level, casting a shadow over their immediate locality. The Zoning Resolution required that in the construction of a skyscraper the building envelope, its profile, must be set back as it rises along a line at least as shallow as an imaginary hypotenuse (the longest side of a right-angled triangle) as drawn from the apex of the building to the base of the structure if projected to the opposite side of the street. This defined the building's mass as it rose and effectively imposed on each set of floors a series recessed step-backs, not unlike a Mayan stepped pyramid.

The result of the Zoning Resolution was to check overnight the indiscriminate construction of tall buildings, the effect of which compromised the amount of light that reached adjacent buildings. It partly determined the distinctive shape of the Empire State Building, compelling the new building's architect, Lamb, to introduce the first of a series of step-backs at 6th-floor level, another at the 30th floor, and another at the 86th floor. The Zoning Resolution's federal successor, the Standard State Zoning Enabling Act of 1926, imposed similar disciplines on buildings in other cities, such as the remarkable Palmolive Building (1929), designed by Holabird & Root, on Michigan Avenue, Chicago, complete with its Lindbergh beacon lamp atop the skyscraper, shining out over Lake Michigan.

Raymond Hood acknowledged the Zoning Law with his application of step-backs in his design for the Daily News Building, 1930. Interestingly, this building is a hybrid between the Empire State Building and the RCA Building (fig. 46, p.96), in that it emphasises verticality, and helps demonstrate why the Zoning Law was eventually repealed. Other buildings applying the style are the First National Center in Oklahoma City and Battersea Power Station in London (see left-hand figure, fig. 23, p.59). Despite the impact of the Zoning Resolution on the New York skyline, it remained imperfect and was eventually replaced in 1960, having been amended some 1,500 times since 1916!

Fig. 43.

Empire State Building New York,
1932, Shreeve Lamb & Harmon

The Empire State building rises through
102 storeys and culminates in a metal
grid communications mast. Its façade is
of Indiana limestone. It remained the
tallest skyscraper in the world for decades.
The name originates from that given to the
State of New York, the Empire State.

The Zoning Resolution's limitations represented a creative challenge to architects, and were dealt with in a particularly imaginative way by Raymond Hood in building the Radio Corporation of America's Building, part of the Columbia University owned Rockefeller Center (1930–9), a complex of four huge buildings in midtown Manhattan privately developed by yet another industrialist titan, John D. Rockefeller, President of the Standard Oil Corporation (Esso). The RCA Building's design fell just the right side of what was justifiable under the code's stipulations, as is evident in the slablike appearance of this remarkable structure. Rising to 70 storeys, the building resembles not so much a tower as it does a slab of stone punctuated with windows and spandrels (the panels connecting two window frames) recessed from the façade. This effect creates elongated vertical ribbing progressing to the top of the tower, lending the building a soaring monumentality.

Skyscrapers, especially icon towers like the Empire State Building and the Chrysler Building, attract corporate tenants very readily because of the obvious projection of corporate strength and success. During the Art Deco era, this pertained not only to the size of the buildings themselves, but also to their opulent decoration in the form of marble and granite stone cladding, bronze door and window frames, and generous external and internal building ornamentation in metal finishes. The same may be true of buildings that punctuate the land creating a landmark especially when they are separate from other similar structures as at the US Federal Bullion Reserve, Kentucky and the Parthenon at the Acropolis both reposing in splendid isolation.

Another remarkable building is the Genesee Valley Trust Building in Rochester, upstate New York. The upper section of this tower is crowned with a massive Art Deco aluminium sculpture comprising four cruciform wings known as the 'Wings of Progress'.

Fig. 44.
Empire State Building, New York, 1932, Shreeve Lamb & Harmon

Detail of the Art Deco shell cladding to the structural members that support the faceted, glazed screens of the upper section of the tower, immediately below the main complex of antennae.

After the Second World War, construction of skyscrapers in the iconic manner abated. Three notable exceptions were Frank Lloyd Wright's Price Tower in Bartlesville, Oklahoma (1953), the construction in 1974 of the tallest skyscraper in the United States, the Sears Tower in Chicago (108 storeys), and the Twin Towers of the World Trade Center in New York just a few years earlier. The remarkable Price Tower, under the supervision of architect Katherine Ririe, was originally destined for the Bowery district in New York's Lower East Side. It is a superb example of varied concrete cantilevered flooring rising through 19 storeys clad with echoes of Art Deco designs in its exterior cast-metal panelling, and remains a treasured landmark in Oklahoma.

Fig. 45.
First National Center, Oklahoma City, 1932, Weary & Alford

This skyscraper, built in the 1930s, was designed in accordance with the New York Zoning Law and repeated the remarkably successful design formula first seen in the Empire State Building.

Fig 46.
Radio Corporation of America
Building, New York, 1935,
Raymond Hood

This building is one of four monolithic
towers creating an urban development
in central Manhattan. The larger of
the four towers is the RCA Building, which
incorporates the Radio City Music Hall,
and dominates the group. The design
of the building, including set-backs to
the building's façade, shows an
imaginative interpretation of New York
City's Zoning Law.

Fig. 47.

Genesee Valley Trust Building,
Rochester, New York, 1930,
Voorhees, Gmelin & Walker

This impressive Art Deco tower is crowned
with four massive sculptured aluminium
wings, known as the 'Wings of Progress',
which dominate the district. The sculpture
is of super-monumental proportions, rising
to over 28m (95ft). When considered in
isolation from the rest of the building,
the masonry form below the sculpture is
reminiscent of mausoleum structures
(see p.16–17).

CHAPTER 7

From Internationalism back to the St Pancras Hotel: relating aesthetically to buildings

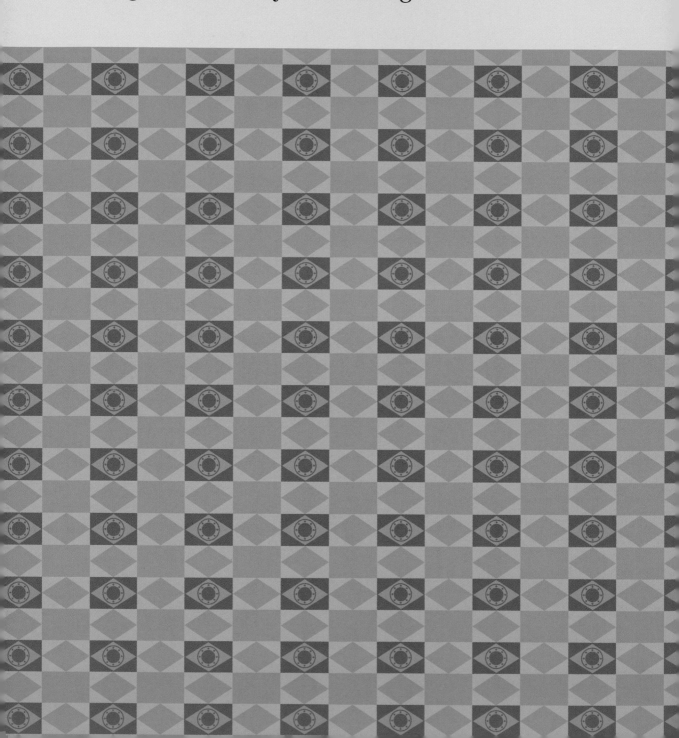

✺ Modernism and the International Style

Modernism, as a state of mind among artists and intellectuals, began in the decade preceding the First World War, and in architecture during the interwar years became the International Style. It represented the desire for a new integrity in architecture, freed from historical precedent, but elements of both the design solutions and the materials used by the modernists had their origins elsewhere. Glazed exterior curtain walling, for instance, a favourite modernist trait, was seen at the Crystal Palace as early as 1851, while ferroconcrete was a late 19th-century development used by August Perret (1874–1954) on an apartment block in the Rue Franklin in Paris in 1903. The iron frame, around which was built the St Pancras Hotel in London in 1867, became the steel frame of the Chicago School used on the early skyscrapers.

These elements came together at Gropius's Fagus Works (1911–13), built of reinforced concrete and glazed surfaces that appear to float unsupported by any framing. This building, amongst others, defined the new course for modernism, later endorsed by the Bauhaus concept of 1925. The modern movement was seen as being able to deliver a new architecture based on glass, steel and concrete, creating a minimalist, uncluttered elegance in space through the use of lightweight materials such as glass and steel and even concrete structures by Robert Maillart (1872–1940), such as the gasoline station on p.54.

The Bauhaus held sway over design issues in Europe during the interwar years. In 1930 Mies van der Rohe became its Director until it closed in 1933. Eleven years previously he had designed a building in Berlin 20 storeys in height with exterior glazed curtain walling. This glass skyscraper did eventually find form, though not in Berlin but in New York as the Seagram Building (completed in 1958), following the first application of the style in Mies's residential towers along Lake Shore Drive in Chicago (1949–51).

The modern movement also addressed residential schemes in concrete, such as the numerous cubic houses designed by French architect Robert Mallet-Stevens in the 1920s. Indeed Erich Mendelsohn (1887–53), the designer of the famous Einstein Tower in Berlin (1919–21), also built houses in England including one in Old Church Street, Chelsea in London, whilst working on his steel and glass curved De La Warr Pavilion at Bexhill-on-Sea, England (1935). Fig. 48 (p.100), a private house in Newbury, England designed by Sir John Burnett in 1929 shows the English approach to modernist housing. The early modernists had also designed residences, among them Adolf Loos's Steiner House in Vienna (1910) and Hoffmann's Stoclet Palace.

Towards the end of the 1930s many architects left Europe to settle in the United States. As well as van der Rohe, Mendelsohn, Gropius and Saarinen, another émigré, Rudolf Schindler (1887–1953), achieved notoriety with his distinctive large

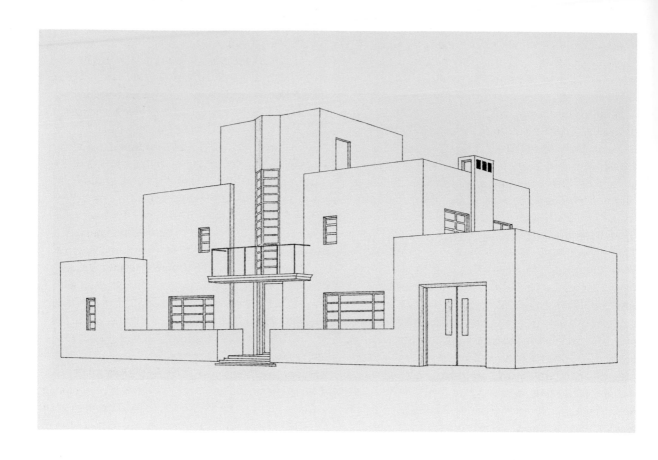

Fig. 48.

Private Residence, Newbury,
Berkshire, 1929, Sir John Burnet

This cement-finished structure, based
on a cubic pyramid, shows the English
approach to modernism in housing. The
building is made up of clean horizontal and
vertical elements, allowing spatial access
to the various roofs and integral balcony.

houses of glass and white concrete walls in California and also his association for a while with Frank Lloyd Wright.

A giant in American architecture, Wright was originally apprenticed to the draughting offices of Louis Sullivan (1856–1924) in Chicago. He did more to develop the American vernacular style of architecture than anyone else, a manner expressed in numerous private houses from the Robie House in Chicago (1908–10) to Fallingwater (1935–37) in Pennsylvania. Though not confined to domestic architecture, Wright was able to transfer design elements from commercial buildings – notably the Larkin Building (1904–06) in Buffalo, NY – such as three-dimensional geometric shapes and column symbols, to later residential buildings such as his Hollyhock House in California (1919–21). Other pioneering examples of Modernist design in domestic building in the United States were M.J. Black's Mansion House in California (1935; fig. 50, p.103), and G. Kraetch's Butler House in Des Moines, Iowa (1935; fig. 49, p.102).

As early as 1904 Wright applied geometric shapes based on Mayan art when designing the Larkin Building, which were repeated later on his Midway Gardens in Chicago (1913) and on the Imperial Hotel in Tokyo (1915–22). Wright continued to apply this idiom of geometric shaping in the form of a series of cantilevers created by the overhang of each floor and disguised by exterior glazed curtain walling as at the Johnson Wax Research Tower at Racine, Wisconsin (1936). This successful innovation was the prelude to Wright's Price Tower in Bartlesville, Oklahoma, which explored the effect of varied cantilevered flooring through 19 storeys.

In the early 1950s buildings of steel and concrete were designed, with the focus on simplicity and little or no ornamentation. Such a direct, brutal approach to style, devoid of any compassion in detailing or any desire to relate to the observer, was the hallmark of the internationalist style that evolved from early modernism. An example of this brutalism can be found at the Barbican complex in London, begun in 1965 as an urban development, and designed by Chamberlin, Powell and Bon. The word 'barbican' describes the outer defence of a fortified city from the Middle Ages, an apt choice of name for such a stylistically uncompromising development. Here brutalism is clearly expressed in the heavy use of massive units of poured concrete dressed in pebbledash finish, creating a very harsh, seemingly destruction-proof texture. Designed at the height of brutalism's influence, the Barbican's design criteria are manifest in other, earlier urban renewal projects such as the Southbank Centre in London, built by Denys Lasdun (1914–2001), and the Lincoln Center in New York.

Some of the ideals of the modern movement emerged in the 1920s, and its aims to some extent were influenced as a direct result of the horrors of the Great War. Many felt that the war could have been avoided had there been a more democratic political system that was responsive to public concern. Naturally enough this led to a review of the prevailing political and social regimes. In addition, even before the war was over an influenza pandemic had erupted that lasted a year and killed more people across the globe than had died in the war itself. Partly as a result of this natural tragedy, hygiene and clean, sleek surfaces were uppermost in designers' minds, especially those who welcomed the production of easily prefabricated buildings constructed of disease-resistant clean materials such as glass, steel and concrete. This approach to designing was taken up by various architects including Le Corbusier, Gropius and Adolph Schneck, and also Aalto on his various sanatorium schemes.

The modern movement developed into the International Style after yet another world war as a generation of radical young designers were able to thrive in the new, more meritocratic atmosphere of the 1950s and 1960s. To be radical was their creed. The internationalists

Fig. 49.

Butler House, Des Moines, Iowa,
1935, G. Kraetch

This example of a streamlined modernist
house was designed by G. Kraetch in
conjunction with the building owner,
E.E. Butler. The building demonstrates the
successful juxtaposition of curved sections
and straight lines – a common feature
of 1930s American domestic architecture.

Fig. 50.
Mansion House, California,
1935, M.J. Black

This 1935 white-painted, cement-finished
residential building emphasises access
to the various flat surfaces in the form
of verandas and roofs. This building
represents the dominant Moderne domestic
style pervading California at this time.

began by promoting extreme design solutions and their dogmatic approach produced inert blank buildings with all the flair of the concrete slab. Often the slab was the salient feature of their designs complete with paraphernalia that appears to be at variance with the original designs. In an attempt to reduce ornamentation and create clean lines, materials are often used that are unsuited to the structure and inappropriate for their purpose – such as plastic laminated boards that will delaminate and bleach when subject to the actions of rain and sunlight. A popular reaction to buildings created by the internationalists is one of disappointment and which today shows no sign of diminishing.

The new British Library building in London, by architect Colin St John Wilson completed in 1997, demonstrates these points precisely, even more so given that it is located adjacent to the St Pancras Hotel, where a sharp contrast in design approach can be observed. The construction of the British Library took over 25 years to complete. The designs and construction programmes were subject to political interference by whatever government held office at the time as is evident in the fact that the published model of the proposed building bears little resemblance of the constructed edifice. Given the colossal budget and the resources available to the architects to build the library, the results are disappointing.

The front of the building, which addresses a very important thoroughfare, the Euston Road, was designed with a low-quality brick façade complete with metal window paraphernalia. Vertical sections of this blank brick wall are joined together with intumescent plastic seal strips about 60mm (2¼in.) wide. This would be an acceptable way to build a low-cost brick warehouse but not a prominent national building. When the building was eventually finished, over-budget, it was found that the internal operation of the Library, including the crucial book-retrieval system, was below standard. More importantly, the facility to

be able to store the Library's full collection of books on site for easy reference was found to be inadequate. The book storage capacity – the basic rationale of the building in locating all books on one site, had simply failed. The building does not execute its primary function as an operating library because of weaknesses in the response to the initial design brief.

By contrast, the complex of towers at Canary Wharf erected at the same time demonstrate that the principles of modern architecture can be applied successfully. This is also evident at Bishopsgate, where the intention has been not to dismiss modern international architecture, but rather to focus on the clarity of design process. This is true of a wide spectrum of post-war buildings, from Michael Graves's Portland Public Service Building in Oregon (1980–83) to James Stirling's School of Engineering at Leicester University (1959–63), which follows the true modernist style of the Bauhaus in its innovative use of glass and steel.

The British Library is not the only modern building in the Euston Road in London that fails to attract praise. A short walk along the same road to the west reveals another structure that was also the result of interference in the development of railway stations by a British Prime Minister, in this case Harold Macmillan. He sanctioned the demolition of the original Euston Railway Station in London and its famous grand entrance in the form of a massive Doric arch modelled on the Propylaea in Athens. Both the arch and the original station, built in 1837–38 by Philip Hardwick (1792–1870), were torn down in 1962 and replaced with a modern building that displays all the bleakest aspects of the International Style. Various commentators, including the former Poet Laureate Sir John Betjeman, have remarked upon this building, which perhaps explains the emergence of the Georgian Group and Victorian Society in England (founded in 1937 and 1958 respectively), created to give expression to a growing public dismay at this type of design. Subsequently, Euston Station

Fig. 51.

Euston Railway Station, London, 1968, Richard Seifert

An interpretation of the modern, functional railway station built in the International style. This building replaced the previous station designed in the classical style in 1837–38 by Philip Hardwick. The opening of the station coincided with the commencement of the Victorian age. The Brutalist architecture of the replacement structure took no inspiration from the previous building, the architects instead declaring, 'simplicity is the keynote in design of the new Euston!'.

is as architecturally bankrupt as it is unpopular with the rail passengers compelled to use it.

The original station was centred on its Great Hall, the inspiration for the halls of both Grand Central Terminal and the Pennsylvania Railroad Station, in New York. As with most railway stations being built at the time, including St Pancras Station a few years later, the London & Birmingham Railway was keen to make a grand statement to passengers using its station. The Doric Arch was over 27m (90ft) high.

It was thought that this magnificent structure had been lost forever, until, in 2004, the masonry blocks that formed the Arch were located in the River Lea in London, where they had been dumped after demolition. Moreover, there is currently increased interest in reconstructing the arch as an aesthetic focal point for a planned urban improvement development at Euston.

The public's reaction to the International Style was based on the perception that the buildings designed according to its tenets did little to improve the surrounding environment. Rather the buildings detracted from the human scale and made being anywhere near them a negative experience. The Lincoln Center (1966) and the Southbank Centre (1951–68) are considered by enthusiasts for the International Style to be triumphs of urban planning and design. By contrast, detractors of the style consider them to be monumental failures that are only still in use today because of the absence of viable alternatives.

The Lincoln Center in New York attracts criticism because of the overuse of concrete. However, this need not be unattractive: the Yale University Arts and Architecture Building (completed 1963) by Paul Rudolph (1918–1997) together with Wright's Fallingwater House in Pennsylvania both make skilful and pleasing use of concrete. The same criticism can be levelled at the Southbank Centre in London, parts of which

were designed by Denys Lasdun, yet the same architect had previously designed the concrete structure that is the University of East Anglia in England successfully.

From the early 1950s until the 1980s office blocks tended to be designed using steel and glass exterior curtain walling. This approach can make economic reason but little aesthetic sense. Two modernist buildings in particular created in the International Style, both commissioned by soap magnates, demonstrate these considerations. Lever House (1952) designed by Skidmore, Owings and Merrill, and the Colgate-Palmolive Building (1955) are both on Park Avenue, New York. With their flat glazed surfaces, both structures reflected the prevailing view of the time that modern buildings needed to be functional, not innovative or interesting. The Colgate-Palmolive building in New York does little to reflect the Palmolive skyscraper in Chicago built some 25 years earlier in the Art Deco style.

The technology and range of building materials available today is extensive. Designs for modern structures using these materials have created some impressive and successful buildings incorporating awesome spans over distances previously unimaginable. There are huge design opportunities with these new materials. Of all the plastic materials, concrete is the most adaptable, facilitating the construction of innovative and interesting structures. The most accomplished have been those that combine concrete with an innovative approach to three-dimensional geometric forms, echoing the early Art Deco profiles. This can be seen at Joplin Railroad Station (fig. 25, p.61). The effect is enhanced in minimalist structures such as fig. 21 (p.54), where all but the most prominent features are trimmed down, creating breathtaking beauty.

Fig. 52.
Doric Arch, Euston, London, 1835,
Philip Hardwick

Originally located in front of Euston
Station, Phillip Hardwick's triumphal
Doric Arch was 92ft (28m) high.
It was demolished in 1963 to make
way for the present railway station.

✿ Bishopsgate: the largest commercial development in Europe

Invariably, corporate commissions tend to place emphasis on visual prestige, the building functioning as a statement about the company. In London one building in particular which expresses corporate prestige is on Bishopsgate, built in 1986–91 by US architects Skidmore, Owings and Merrill. The main pavilion building at Bishopsgate comprises 135 Bishopsgate Phase VI, Bishopsgate Exchange Phase VII and Number 1 Exchange Square Phase VIII, with other phases designed by Arup Associates for Rosehaugh Stanhope Developments.

The building invites the public to share in its space, through the provision of a public colonnade above the sidewalk. In so doing it addresses the street upon which it is constructed, which as we have seen is a classical ideal. The opulent aspect of the building reflects the confident Beaux-Arts style, complete with marble and stone cladding and bronze ornamental finishes, and makes use of colonnades, steps, and light globes in an imaginative way.

In 1985 the de-regulation of financial markets created demand for offices close to the City in London, and Bishopsgate was selected for development. A scheme by English architects, Fitzroy Robinson, proposed the demolition of two Victorian railway stations – a fate that befell Euston Station a decade before (see pp.104–6). Concerned by this potential act of corporate state vandalism, conservationists led by Sir John Betjamin – who had successfully resisted demolition of St Pancras Hotel – opposed this approach. A Public Inquiry was convened and a revised scheme by Rosehaugh Stanhope Developments (now Stanhope plc), was accepted, and Phases I to IV of the designs by Arup were implemented, creating the Broadgate Centre at Bishopsgate.

Because construction time was critical to ensure that the project delivered the office space that was in demand at a financially competitive price, American architects Skidmore Owings & Merrill (SOM) were appointed to complete Phases V to XIV because of their experience in fast-track American construction methods. The construction methods at Bishopsgate were important because they influenced two new approaches – method and management – to the construction industry in the UK.

At this time the demand for the rapid erection of buildings was alien to the conservative UK construction industry, with its traditional methods of construction and procurement practices. This meant the method of off-site pre-fabrication was precluded (despite the fact this technique was developed in England in the 1850s with the iron-framed Crystal Palace, see pp.27–8). While innovative use of the iron frame – applied, for example, in 1867 at St Pancras Hotel in London (see pp.47–9) – allowed builders to erect structures quickly and cheaply, the exterior cladding to buildings, was still carried out by masons, glaziers and carpenters working on-site – occasionally using pre-fabricated elements. Although this approach was expensive and labour intensive, the UK construction industry was reluctant to accept the US model of assembling pre-fabricated pieces on site. This promoted speed of erection and was first demonstrated by the creators of the Empire State Building in New York fifty years earlier, where the rough edges of Indiana limestone panels or window panels were hidden by the aluminium mullions into which they were inserted. At Bishopsgate SOM encouraged contractors to explore new cladding methods, suggesting that composite stone panels and balustrades were made off site, instead of carving the masonry or forming brickwork on site.

The American method of construction management was implemented by SOM and Stanhope plc. Under it, each trade contractor has an equal and direct contractual relationship with the client where no contractor is subservient to another, as a sub-contractor is to a main-contractor. Construction management promoted decisive, pragmatic decision making, saving time and costs making the project economically viable.

While these new approaches in construction method and management were implemented in the Bishopsgate project, the UK construction industry showed its innate conservatism, in its reluctantance to accept the new construction regime. During the 1980s there was resistance in the UK to these American models being used not only at Bishopsgate but also at SOM's project at Canary Wharf, London. Luddite arguments raged in the English architectural press, indicating the deep-rooted prejudices of those who dismissed the American methods. Their inability to understand innovative modern methods was demonstrated at the British Library, built at the same time as Bishopsgate, but massively over budget and behind schedule. Critically, the British Library project also failed to appreciate the client's requirements, and those of the public, for an appropriate design.

The Beaux-Arts-style designs of SOM express economic prestige, and reflect the early 20th century use of this style as an interpretation of Classicism. The Bishopsgate building has an imposing central portico flanked by two smaller porticos at either side connected by an internal elevated colonnade parallel to the street. English architects may feel uncomfortable with, and argue against, massive structures that radiate success and confidence such as those at Bishopsgate or Canary Wharf. However, similar concerns were expressed in the early twentieth century about the creation of skyscrapers in the United States. Comparable structures weren't built in the UK until 1987, which saw the construction of the tallest skyscraper in Europe at Canary Wharf.

Despite architectural reservations expressed in the UK, American construction models triumphed at Bishopsgate and Broadgate, delivering three and a half million square feet of real estate and offices in London – the largest commercial development in Europe. The scheme attracted 33 awards and was visited by Queen Elizabeth II upon its completion. The developer British Land Plc now operates Bishopsgate through its Broadgate Estates.

❖ Revitalising buildings

As a result of advances in building technology and design over the last 200 years or so, many structures have outlived their original purpose but are either prized for their style or deemed inappropriate for a prime location. Consequently, they are either preserved for another function or earmarked for demolition. The Union Pacific Railroad has faced such dilemmas with regard to its own railroad stations and depots throughout the United States. As a consequence of the development of air travel and the automobile, the requirement for rail travel has diminished. Irrespective of any social necessity, railroads are not really a viable economic option save in large metropolitan districts. The Union Pacific Railroad came up with a novel solution when it decided to convert its railroad stations into uptown developments to attract new business opportunities to what were rundown areas following the closure of the railroad stations.

Three such developments are based around the redundant railroad stations at Kansas City, St Louis and Joplin (see figs 27 and 28, pp.61–2), all in Missouri. These former transport hubs have since become the pivots of major developments in the surrounding areas, which have imbued the station buildings with a new vitality. Buildings that had become redundant and would once have been demolished and replaced have been granted a new lease of life for a different use, mainly as a result of environmental and conservation issues that now make it socially unacceptable and uneconomic to demolish old buildings without careful thought. In the mid-20th century, typically, warehouses along the Thames that had no practical or discernible function were torn

Index